PRODUCT LIABILITY IN THE UNITED STATES

A Primer for Manufacturers and Their Employees

LINDA GORDON

D1473183

Product Liability in the United States

➤

A PRIMER FOR MANUFACTURERS

AND THEIR EMPLOYEES

Perkins Coie

Anchorage, Alaska

Bellevue, Washington

Los Angeles, California

Portland, Oregon

Seattle, Washington

Spokane, Washington

Washington, D.C.

This primer is a publication of the Perkins Coie Product Liability Practice Group. Materials herein have been abridged from laws, court decisions and administrative rulings and should not be construed as legal advice or opinions on specific facts. Any questions regarding the contents of this primer may be directed to your contact lawyer at Perkins Coie or to Keith Gerrard, Perkins Coie, 1201 Third Avenue, 40th Floor, Seattle, Washington 98101-3099, (206) 583-8888.

Library of Congress No. 9160104   ISBN No. 1-879650-00-2
Design by Ellen Ziegler Design   Illustrations by David Johnson

CONTENTS

FOREWORD

We are lawyers who defend manufacturers in product liability lawsuits. We have written this primer because our experience has taught us this very important lesson—

Manufacturers are hurt in product liability litigation in the United States because their key employees do not understand the law and the legal process used to obtain damage awards from their employers. Because they lack this information, these employees in their day-to-day actions commit errors that lose lawsuits and increase the amount of damages awarded.

This primer provides basic information about product liability laws and legal procedures in product liability lawsuits in the United States. It also suggests measures that you can take to reduce your product liability exposure.

This primer is intended to be read by your nonlegal personnel. It can be used as a source book for a product liability prevention program or as the syllabus for a more extensive corporate program. We have simplified where possible, but product liability is not a simple subject. This primer will yield its maximum benefit if studied carefully.

We conduct product liability educational seminars for our manufacturing clients because we know that product liability exposure is reduced when the type of information contained in this primer is provided to employees—particularly to managers and other key decision makers. These are the people who make design decisions, determine what product literature or placards are called for, evaluate in-service experience and adopt or reject product improvements. These are also the people who will be called on to testify in American courts in defense of your products. This primer was written for them.

INTRODUCTION

Manufacturers have increasingly had to defend themselves in lawsuits in the United States brought by people who claim to have been injured by defective products. All too often manufacturers lose and end up paying large damage awards. Damage awards in excess of $1 million have become common. Even if a manufacturer successfully defends a product in court, the burdens of time and expense imposed by lawsuits are substantial.

The laws are astonishingly tough. To many they seem unfair. Courts order manufacturers to pay for injuries suffered by consumers who were careless or who misused products. In one such case, a man who was injured while improperly operating a cotton-picking machine recovered a substantial sum of money from the machine's manufacturer. He had tried to dislodge a rock caught in the machine's picking mechanism by kicking it out with his foot, disobeying the manufacturer's clear instructions to shut off the machine before removing obstructions. As the man dislodged the rock, he caught his foot in the cotton picker's moving parts and was severely injured. He sued the manufacturer and argued in court that the cotton picker should have been equipped with emergency power cut-off switches above each of its several picking mechanisms, so that an operator who misused the machine, as he had, could turn it off before becoming too entangled. The manufacturer pointed out that this alteration, quite apart from its cost, would only encourage other operators to repeat the man's mistake. The court, however, agreed with the operator and awarded the man almost half a million dollars.

Many managers and employees of manufacturers are dismayed by the results of such lawsuits. Yet because they don't understand the legal standards used to decide whether a manufacturer must pay for a consumer's injuries, they fail to take steps during the development and production of their products that could reduce the likelihood of future claims or make it easier to defend them. For example, because a manufacturer may have to pay for a consumer's injury even though the consumer used the product carelessly, manufacturers should try to anticipate likely ways in which their products may be misused and then design or label them to discourage misuse or at least minimize its hazardous effects.

Most employees also understand little about lawsuits and, through ignorance, often take actions that harm the manufacturer's ability to defend itself. They may not know that courts give consumers the power to force a manufacturer to disclose vast quantities of documentation and make its employees available for questioning under oath. An employee who does not realize the extent of such disclosure requirements might write a memo after an incident has occurred using language that could later be misinterpreted as admitting the existence of a product defect.

Any effective program to avoid product liability lawsuits and minimize the impact of the lawsuits that inevitably occur requires the manufacturer's nonlegal personnel to have a basic understanding of product liability law and the litigation process. Chapter I of this primer describes basic concepts of product liability law. Chapter II outlines the structure of product liability lawsuits. Chapter III discusses specific steps that a manufacturer can take to reduce its product liability exposure.

At the back of this book is a glossary of terms. There is also a form that you can return to us if you would like to be included on a mailing list for future revisions or updates of this primer.

Note: Masculine pronouns have been used throughout our text for simplicity and are intended to apply to persons of both sexes.

PRODUCT

LIABILITY LAW

➤ 1 ≺

There is really no such thing as "United States product liability law." Each of the 50 states, the District of Columbia and the various territories that make up the United States has its own rules defining the liability of a manufacturer for injuries. These rules have been developed largely by the courts in each state, although state legislatures have enacted statutes that also affect product liability law. Furthermore, on some questions, "federal" law— law enacted by the United States Congress or developed by the United States Supreme Court or other federal courts—will govern. Federal law may govern certain aspects of a case even though other aspects of the case are controlled by the law of one or more of the states.

The laws of the various states differ, sometimes in ways critical to the outcome of a case. As will be discussed at the end of this chapter, deciding which law will apply is often difficult. Nevertheless, the laws of virtually all states have enough in common that some general concepts can be stated. In describing these general concepts, we have made frequent use of the term *plaintiff*. As discussed in Chapter II, the plaintiff is the person who brings a lawsuit seeking an award of damages for an injury. In a product liability lawsuit, the plaintiff can be anyone injured by the product, including a consumer who purchased the product, a user of a product owned by another, or a bystander (such as a pedestrian struck by an automobile). If an accident results in death, the plaintiff may be a representative of the deceased person's estate or surviving family members. The *defendant* is the party the plaintiff sues.

Legal Theories of Liability

Negligence   All states hold a manufacturer responsible for injuries caused by its employees' *negligence.* This means that a manufacturer is legally liable when its employees fail to exercise reasonable care for the safety of potential users of the manufacturer's product. For example, an electrical appliance manufacturer whose employee carelessly fails to connect a grounding wire during manufacture will be liable to a user injured by an electrical shock caused by the ungrounded condition.

Under this negligence theory the manufacturer is treated no differently from other defendants in other types of lawsuits. The surgeon who carelessly performs an operation can be liable to an injured patient. The automobile driver who carelessly injures a pedestrian can also be liable. Similarly, any carelessness or negligence by the manufacturer or its employees that results in an injury can be the basis for liability.

Breach of Warranty   All states also hold a manufacturer legally liable if a product that it says will meet certain standards falls short of those standards and causes injury. The injured person in such cases can sue for *breach of warranty.* There are several ways in which a warranty can be created. To begin with, many manufacturers provide a written warranty with each product sold or include a warranty provision in the contract for the sale of the product. A warranty can also be implied by law or by the circumstances of the sale. The usual warranty implied by law is that the product is suitable for the ordinary purposes for which it will be used. This includes an implied promise that the product does not have any defects that would render it dangerous. A warranty can also be created by representations contained in advertisements promoting the product.

Thirty years ago, breach of warranty claims were common, and many courts allowed such claims to be asserted against a manufacturer with whom the plaintiff had never had any direct dealings. The plaintiff did not have to prove that the manufacturer had been careless, but only that the product failed to perform as promised in the manufacturer's express or implied warranty. Consequently, from the plaintiff's standpoint, a breach of warranty claim was generally preferable to a negligence claim. There were some potential disadvantages for the plaintiff, however, such as the fact that a breach of warranty lawsuit was barred unless started within four years from the date of sale.

Today, breach of warranty is a much less important theory. With the adoption of the legal doctrine of strict liability, discussed below, many courts have come to recognize that the breach of warranty theory should be reserved for contract claims between parties to contracts for the sale of goods in which the buyer has suffered commercial losses. Nevertheless, product liability lawsuits by injured consumers routinely include a separate claim for breach of warranty.

Strict Liability   In addition to negligence and warranty law, nearly all states have adopted a standard commonly called *strict liability* for the sale of defective products. The most common model for strict liability is a standard proposed over 25 years ago by a group of legal scholars, lawyers and judges. That standard, commonly called "Section 402A" because it was published as Section 402A of a legal treatise, states:

> *(1) One who sells any product in a defective condition unreasonably dangerous to the user or consumer or to his property is subject to liability for physical harm thereby caused to the ultimate user or consumer, or to his property, if*
>> *(a) the seller is engaged in the business of selling such a product, and*
>> *(b) it is expected to and does reach the user or consumer without substantial change in the condition in which it is sold.*
> *(2) The rule stated in subsection (1) applies although*
>> *(a) the seller has exercised all possible care in the preparation and sale of his product, and*
>> *(b) the user or consumer has not bought the product from or entered into any contractual relation with the seller.*

To hold a manufacturer responsible on a strict liability claim, the plaintiff must prove that *(a)* the product was defective, *(b)* the defect existed at the time the manufacturer delivered the product and *(c)* the defect caused the plaintiff's injuries.

Although strict liability evolved from breach of warranty law, it offers a plaintiff significant advantages over breach of warranty law by eliminating defenses that had been applied by some courts (e.g., the requirement that there be a contractual relationship between the plaintiff and the manufacturer and the requirement that warranty claims be brought within a specified period, typically four years from the date of sale of the product). Thus, for example, a pedestrian injured in an automobile accident can sue the manufacturer directly, and the manufacturer would not have defenses based on its lack of a contractual relationship with the pedestrian or on the fact that it had sold the automobile more than four years earlier.

Strict liability also offers the plaintiff significant advantages over the negligence standard because it relieves the plaintiff of the burden of proving that the defendant or its employees acted without due care. As stated in Section 402A, it is no defense to a consumer's strict liability lawsuit that the manufacturer exercised all possible care. If a jury believes that the product delivered by the manufacturer was defectively manufactured, the manufacturer will be liable for any injury caused by the product, no matter how careful it was to avoid the defect.

Types of Defects

Under any of the three theories of liability discussed above, the plaintiff generally can recover damages only if the product is found to be defective. There are three different types of defects that a product may have: a defect in manufacturing, in design and in warning or instruction.

Manufacturing Defects   The concept of a manufacturing defect is the easiest to explain. A product has a manufacturing defect when it is not built according to its specifications and is consequently unsafe. For example, during manufacture an employee might forget to tighten a nut, or there might be a hidden flaw in the metal from which the product is made. These would be manufacturing defects.

Design Defects   A design defect is much more difficult to define because there is no clear standard against which the product can be evaluated. (As explained in later sections, compliance with government and industry design standards is not enough to avoid liability for design defects, but violation of such standards is likely to result in liability.) A few courts have said that the concept of "design defect" is no more than negligent design. According to those courts, the question in a design case is whether the manufacturer used reasonable care in designing the product.

Most courts reject that approach and say that defective design is something different from (and generally easier to prove than) negligent design. These courts generally say that a product is defectively designed if the product is more dangerous than an ordinary consumer would expect or if the benefits of the product's design do not outweigh its risks. For example, if a power lawnmower is sold without a guard to protect the user from being struck by ejected items, the mower might be considered defective either because it failed to meet consumer expectations or because risk-benefit considerations dictate that a guard should have been installed.

Warning and Instruction Defects   A warning or instruction defect exists when the product's manual, instruction booklet, packaging, labels or placards fail to provide adequate warnings of possible dangers associated with the product or instructions regarding its safe use. For example, a drug may be defective despite its beneficial effects if the manufacturer fails to issue adequate warnings to consumers regarding side effects. In a defective warning case, a court will determine whether the manufacturer's warning reasonably advised the user of the hazards associated with the product. Many courts say that it is not a defense that the manufacturer did not know of the hazard. The manufacturer may be held liable even if the hazard was unknowable at the time of manufacture due to technological limitations.

Proof of Defect

A plaintiff normally must prove that the product was defective, that the defect existed at the time of manufacture and that the defect caused his injury. However, following the lead of California, a frequent innovator in product liability law, a few states require the manufacturer to prove the adequacy of the product's design. The plaintiff typically relies on various types of evidence to establish the product's defective condition.

Expert Opinions   Typically, a plaintiff will hire a technical expert to testify about the defective characteristics of a product. Such experts are readily available in the United States. In fact, offering opinions in product liability lawsuits has become the principal business of hundreds of technical experts. It is shameful and discouraging, but nevertheless true, that a plaintiff's attorney can *always* find a university professor, medical doctor, engineer or other industry expert to testify that any product is defective. Most courts are very liberal in permitting such "experts" to testify. The manufacturer's best response is to retain highly qualified experts to rebut the plaintiff's expert testimony and to educate the defense attorney so well that his cross-examination can demolish the plaintiff's "expert."

Manufacturer's Employees and Records   A plaintiff will often use the manufacturer's own records or the testimony of the manufacturer's current or former employees to prove product defect. If the manufacturer's own employees expressed concerns about the product's safety, which were not properly addressed, this can be extremely persuasive that a product defect existed.

Government and Industry Standards   Government agencies and industry associations issue standards applicable to the design and labeling of various types of products. Evidence that the manufacturer's product violates such a standard applicable at the time of manufacture can be compelling proof of the existence of a defect. Violation of a mandatory government regulatory standard results in an automatic finding of negligence in most states.

Similar Incidents   A plaintiff may try to show that the product has caused other similar accidents. The courts have wide discretion in deciding whether to allow evidence of other accidents to be presented at trial. In theory, the burden is on the plaintiff to show substantial similarity between the accidents, but in practice it may become the manufacturer's burden to show that the other accidents were not similar to the plaintiff's.

Government Reports Another type of evidence that a plaintiff may use is a government report commenting on the safety of the product. In most courts, reports setting forth the "factual findings" of an official investigation are admissible as evidence. In federal courts, a statement by a government investigator that most people would view as an "opinion" may be admissible as a factual finding.

Post-Accident Product Changes A plaintiff may attempt to present evidence of a change in design or warning made by the manufacturer as a result of the accident. Such changes may be considered evidence that the original design or warnings were deficient. An unsophisticated jury is certainly likely to draw that inference. There is substantial disagreement among the courts about whether evidence of a post-accident corrective measure should be admissible as evidence. The rule in many federal and state courts is that this evidence should *not* be allowed to prove negligence or the existence of a product defect, the rationale being that admitting this evidence would discourage defendants from making needed safety changes. However, these courts may permit the evidence to be admitted for other purposes, such as to show the feasibility of alternate designs. In addition, a number of other courts have concluded that in a strict liability case this evidence should be admitted to prove the existence of a product defect as well as for other purposes.

Who Is Liable for a Product Defect?

In most states any person engaged in the business of selling or leasing products for use or consumption can be held liable for distributing a defective product. Thus, liability extends to everyone in the chain of distribution from the manufacturer to the retailer. Strict liability applies only if the defendant was in the business of selling the product; it does not apply to occasional sellers who do not market the product as an ordinary part of their business. But even these occasional sellers can be held liable for their own negligence in selling a product if they knew or should have discovered that the product had a dangerous defect.

A number of states have enacted statutes that make strict liability applicable only to manufacturers. Under such statutes retailers and other product sellers are liable only for their own negligence or breach of warranty.

In some instances a plaintiff may have been injured by a generic product, such as a drug, but is unable to identify which of several manufacturers actually made the product that caused the injury. In these rare cases, a few courts have held that all sellers of a defective generic product are liable to the plaintiff and that the award to the plaintiff should be allocated among members of the industry in proportion to their market shares at the time the product was purchased.

Defenses to Liability

The best way to defend a product liability claim successfully at trial is to convince the judge or jury that the product is not defective. However, there are also *affirmative defenses*—defenses that, if proven by the manufacturer, may eliminate or lessen the manufacturer's liability regardless of whether the product has been or could be shown to be defective.

While the liability standards are generally similar from state to state, the affirmative defenses available to a manufacturer vary considerably. The four most important categories of defenses are discussed below:

Plaintiff's Carelessness or Misuse of the Product There is wide variation among the laws of different states regarding whether the plaintiff's own careless conduct is a complete or partial defense. The same is true with respect to the plaintiff's *misuse* of the product, a term which refers to any use of the product that is not in accord with the manufacturer's intended use. In a few states, any careless conduct or misuse by the plaintiff is a complete defense for the manufacturer, without regard to whether the claim is based on negligence, warranty or strict liability. In most states, whether and to what extent the careless conduct or misuse by the plaintiff is a defense depends on the nature of the plaintiff's conduct and the theory of liability asserted against the manufacturer.

If a consumer sues a manufacturer for negligence and the consumer's own negligence contributed to causing the injury, the consumer's recovery will be reduced or eliminated, depending on the state. Under the rule of *contributory negligence* (which historically had widespread application and today survives in some states), any negligence by the plaintiff that helped cause his own injury will bar all recovery from the defendant, regardless of the degree to which it may also be at fault.

Over the past several decades, most states have abandoned contributory negligence and have adopted a rule of *comparative negligence*, under which the jury assigns percentages, totaling 100 percent, to the negligence of the plaintiff and each defendant that caused the injury. Recovery is then reduced based on the plaintiff's percentage. If a plaintiff is 40 percent responsible for the injury, the recovery from the negligent defendants will be reduced by 40 percent. Some states provide that a plaintiff whose negligence is greater than 50 percent cannot recover anything; other states allow a plaintiff some recovery no matter how high his percentage of the total negligence.

When a plaintiff proceeds on a warranty or strict liability theory, there are also varying approaches to whether the plaintiff's own negligence will affect his ability to recover. In some states, any lack of care by the plaintiff will reduce or eliminate the manufacturer's liability. In other states, the plaintiff's recovery is reduced or eliminated only if the plaintiff used a defective product while aware of its defective state or misused the product in a manner unforeseeable to the manufacturer. Many courts say that a plaintiff's misuse that is reasonably foreseeable by the manufacturer is not a complete defense. A manufacturer who sells a chair may not intend for anyone to stand on it, but a jury could easily conclude that such a misuse is reasonably foreseeable.

Alteration or Misuse by Someone Other Than the Plaintiff An injury may occur because of the alteration or misuse of a product by persons other than the manufacturer or the plaintiff. In the past, most courts agreed that any such alteration or misuse eliminated the manufacturer's liability. Now many courts say that such an alteration will defeat liability only if it was not reasonably foreseeable by the manufacturer. Some courts hold the manufacturer liable even when the alteration is the only reason for the defect—removing a safety guard originally installed by the manufacturer, for example.

Alterations can be viewed as one type of misuse of the product. Other forms of misuse by persons other than the plaintiff are frequently analyzed using the same foreseeability approach.

Passage of Time An injured consumer does not have unlimited time to claim damages for his injuries. The legislatures of every state have enacted *statutes of limitations* to protect defendants against stale claims. These statutes impose deadlines, which vary from state to state and typically range from one to six years. Normally, in negligence and strict liability cases, the time period begins to run on the date the plaintiff was injured. In some cases, though, a plaintiff may not immediately become aware of an injury or the cause of the injury. In such cases, many states provide that the time period does not start to run until the plaintiff discovers or reasonably should discover the injury and its cause. In such states, if the discovery does not occur until decades after the plaintiff is harmed by the product—as may be the case with some pharmaceutical and chemical products—the consumer can still bring a product liability claim.

Statutes of limitations that start to run on or after the date of injury give little protection to manufacturers whose products are in use long after they were delivered. Claims with respect to industrial machinery frequently arise from injuries suffered 40 or 50 years after the product was sold. Although such a claim is certainly "stale" in terms of the manufacturer's ability to defend its design decisions, it will not be barred by the statute of limitations as long as the lawsuit is brought within the time limit after the date of the injury.

In response to this situation, a few states have enacted *statutes of repose*. Under such laws a manufacturer is not liable for injuries occurring more than a specified length of time after the product was first delivered by the manufacturer. The time period is typically 10 years or more. Some states do not specify a time period but require instead that the jury determine the "useful safe life" of the particular product. The future of these statutes of repose is uncertain. Several courts have declared such statutes violate constitutional rights by depriving plaintiffs of their claims.

As noted previously, statutes of limitations applicable to warranty claims typically start to run when the product is delivered and expire after four years.

Contract Provisions Some manufacturers include provisions in the contract of sale purporting to disclaim or limit any liability for defects in the product. Contractual *disclaimers* will not prevent a consumer from recovering for personal injuries. They can bar claims for property damage or commercial loss. The precise circumstances under which disclaimers are enforceable outside the personal injury context are complex and highly variable from state to state.

Another defense based on contract provisions may apply when the manufacturer supplied the product to the federal government under a contract that included design specifications. This defense is called the *government-contract-specification defense.* Although the federal government can be liable for personal injuries caused by the negligence of government employees in certain circumstances, it is immune from liability for its discretionary decisions in specifying the design of products it purchases. As a result, courts have decided that the manufacturer should not be liable for personal injuries caused by design defects in the product if *(a)* the federal government approved reasonably precise contract specifications, *(b)* the product conformed to those specifications and *(c)* the manufacturer warned the government about any dangers in the use of the product that were known to the manufacturer but not to the government. The scope of this defense is still being defined by the courts. For example, one court has said that while the defense bars a design defect claim, it does not bar a claim that the manufacturer should have warned ultimate users of the product about the hazard by means of appropriate labeling. Another issue regarding applicability of this defense arises where the government purchases a product that is based on one previously developed for the nongovernment market.

While compliance with government contract specifications can be a defense to liability, compliance with government regulations is generally not a defense. Courts typically view such regulations as establishing minimum standards that the manufacturer may need to exceed to avoid liability.

Damages

Compensatory Damages for Personal Injury and Death   When a manufacturer is found liable to the plaintiff, the plaintiff is entitled to an award of money as compensation for his loss. This is called an award of *compensatory damages.* Until recently, the uniform practice in all American courts was to award damages in a lump sum for all losses, both those incurred before trial and those anticipated after trial. Recently, a handful of states have enacted statutes providing for periodic payments of anticipated post-trial losses.

Damages are typically awarded for both economic and noneconomic losses. *Economic losses* are the actual out-of-pocket expenses and monetary losses that have been or will be incurred by a plaintiff because of his injuries. *Noneconomic losses* are the nonfinancial hardships that have been or will be experienced by the plaintiff (and sometimes by the spouse or other family members). An award of damages for noneconomic losses attempts to translate these hardships into a monetary amount. Some state legislatures have attempted to limit the maximum amount that can be awarded for noneconomic losses. Several of these statutes have been declared unconstitutional by the courts.

When the plaintiff is an individual suing for *personal injury,* the recovery generally will have three elements. First, the plaintiff may recover any earnings he has lost or will lose because of the injury, either from an inability to work or from a diminished capacity to work. Second, the plaintiff may recover the expenses that have been or will be incurred as a result of the injury, including the cost of medical treatment. Third, the plaintiff may recover for mental and physical pain and suffering. The translation of human pain and suffering into an amount of money is necessarily an arbitrary procedure, and the amounts awarded in different cases vary significantly. For each of these three elements, the plaintiff is compensated for past and anticipated future losses.

When a person dies of injuries caused by a product, most states provide two distinct rights of action against the manufacturer. The first is a *survival action,* consisting of any claims that the person could have brought up to the time of his death but did not. For example, the estate of a person who dies of food poisoning 30 days after eating contaminated food may recover for the lost earnings, medical expenses and pain and suffering during the time between injury and death. Many states permit a recovery for pain and suffering even though the deceased lived only for a few minutes after sustaining the injury. In some states a recovery can be had for mental pain and suffering in contemplation of impending death.

The second action that can be brought is a *wrongful death action,* in which the measure of recovery is the economic (and, in most states, noneconomic) losses that surviving family members and other heirs have suffered or will suffer as a result of the death. The major item of damages in such an action is the amount that the heirs would have received in economic support from the deceased if death had not occurred. Lost economic support is typically calculated in this way:

> *Present value of what the deceased would have earned*
> — *Present value of what he would have spent for his own personal consumption*
> ———————————————————————————————————————
> *Lost economic support*

Other economic losses include funeral expenses, the value of the services that the deceased provided to his family and, in some states, any lost inheritance. In states that allow the heirs to recover noneconomic damages, the usual award is for loss of the deceased's "society and companionship." In a few states, the heirs may recover for their own mental anguish caused by the death.

In suits for personal injury or wrongful death, an increasing number of jurisdictions adjust an award for lost earnings or support by considering taxes that the deceased would have had to pay on his earnings. This is appropriate because damage awards in the United States are not subject to income taxes even though the earnings they are intended to replace would have been taxable.

Frequently a plaintiff obtains other compensation for his injury. Examples are health and life insurance policies, pensions, workers' compensation awards and Social Security. In virtually all states, damages are not reduced because of the amounts the plaintiff receives from these *collateral sources*. Rather, the manufacturer must pay the full amount of the damages that the plaintiff has suffered. A well-insured plaintiff can wind up with a substantial economic windfall.

The prevailing party in a lawsuit in the United States generally does not recover any compensation for money paid to the lawyers hired to bring or defend the lawsuit. A prevailing party may recover some court costs, usually a small portion of the entire legal bill. In some states, if the plaintiff's suit is found to be clearly frivolous, the defendant may recover its full expenses, but this rarely occurs in a product liability lawsuit.

Punitive Damages In certain situations, most states permit an award of *punitive damages* in addition to compensatory damages. Punitive damages, as the term indicates, are intended to punish the defendant for the actions on which its liability was based and to deter the defendant and others from acting similarly in the future. Consistent with this purpose, a number of states provide that defendants, *not* their insurers, must pay punitive damage awards.

Most jurisdictions permit punitive damage awards only if the defendant's acts are proven to be particularly egregious, wanton, willful or reckless. Punitive damages are most typically awarded against a manufacturer when the plaintiff can show that a safety hazard was known to the manufacturer and the manufacturer did nothing about it.

The amount of punitive damages is determined by considering both the nature of the defendant's misconduct and the amount necessary to punish the defendant. Consequently, evidence of the defendant's net worth and income often is considered relevant.

The possibility of punitive damage awards has become a matter of deep concern to manufacturers in recent years. Although punitive damage awards still occur in only a few cases, plaintiffs' attorneys have become increasingly adept at portraying even good faith business decisions as evidence of willful disregard for the safety of consumers. Because punitive damage awards are often substantially larger than compensatory damage awards, the potential of a punitive damage award may significantly raise the settlement value of a case. The possibility of receiving a punitive damage award might even lead a plaintiff to pursue a case in which the potential compensatory damages are not large. One particularly troubling aspect of punitive damages is the risk of multiple awards, where the same conduct results in multiple injuries and multiple lawsuits.

Sample Verdicts Because many product liability lawsuits involve multiple claims and several defendants, jury verdicts can range anywhere from a verdict in favor of all defendants on all claims to one against all defendants on all claims. A plaintiff could also prevail on some but not all of his claims against only one, some or all of the defendants.

When the defendant prevails on all claims, the plaintiff is not entitled to any recovery. A prevailing plaintiff is awarded sums of money for compensatory and sometimes punitive damages. The damage awards vary greatly from jurisdiction to jurisdiction. Generally speaking, awards are higher in large urban areas in which the cost of living and salaries are high. Judges and juries in rural areas generally give lower awards for similar injuries. There are, of course, many exceptions to this rule of thumb. More important in determining the amount of an award is the nature of the injury in question, the plaintiff's age and, if the injury impairs the plaintiff's ability to pursue his profession, the plaintiff's earning potential and the extent to which other persons depend on the plaintiff for support. The amount of punitive damages, if any, depends on the nature of the defendant's conduct and finances.

The following are a few sample verdicts and settlements that are included to show not only the possible size of American jury verdicts, but also the factors that may have influenced them:

➤ *A $550,000 verdict in favor of a 65-year-old farmer for the loss of four fingers of his right hand, a fractured forearm and a bleeding ulcer incurred during hospitalization. The injury was caused by farm machinery with a defective gear guard that permitted the plaintiff's hand to become caught in the gears. The verdict was rendered by a jury in a midsized city in the rural Midwest.*

➤ *A $3,360,000 verdict in favor of a woman who sustained third-degree burns over 30 percent of the front of her body, as well as permanent thermal injuries to her upper respiratory tract, when the terry-cloth robe she was wearing caught fire. The verdict against the robe's manufacturer was returned by a jury in a large West Coast city.*

➤ *An $8,500,000 verdict for the deaths of three men flying in a private airplane that broke up in flight. The plaintiffs were their survivors—the wife and two children of a 36-year-old man, the wife and eight children of a 42-year-old man and the two children of a 20-year-old man. The action was brought against the aircraft's manufacturer, alleging defective aircraft design and manufacture. The verdict was rendered by a jury in a midsized city in the industrial Great Lakes area.*

➤ *A $1,590,000 settlement in favor of a press-brake operator who suffered traumatic amputation of three fingers on her right hand and four fingers on her left hand. The lawsuit was filed in a large Midwestern city.*

➤ *A $330,000 verdict against an airline in favor of a 34-year-old executive secretary whose knee was damaged by the failure of an aircraft seat during takeoff. The verdict was awarded by a jury in a large East Coast city.*

➤ A $7,150,000 verdict in favor of the driver and passenger of a small truck involved in a one-vehicle accident caused by a fracture of a defectively manufactured axle. The defendant was the manufacturer of the truck. The plaintiff passenger, who was six weeks old and was riding in a government-approved child safety seat, sustained closed-head injuries that left her permanently retarded, partially blind and physically impaired. She was awarded $5,000,000. Her mother, who was driving the truck, suffered multiple injuries to her legs and pelvis and was awarded $2,000,000. Her husband received $150,000 for loss of consortium (marital association). The verdict was rendered by a jury in a rural county in the South.

➤ A $13,473,588 verdict against a forklift manufacturer in favor of a 19-year-old steelworker who became paralyzed when his forklift slid off the edge of an access road and overturned onto him. The jury found the forklift manufacturer 80 percent negligent and the plaintiff's employer 20 percent negligent. Rendered by a jury in a small town in the rural Midwest, the verdict included a $7,700,000 punitive damage award.

➤ A $4,060,000 verdict against the manufacturer of a wheel loader in favor of a 27-year-old welder who became a paraplegic when pinned beneath the loader when its service brakes failed and it went out of control. The verdict was awarded by a jury in a midsized industrial city in the predominantly rural Southwest.

➤ A $4,138,000 verdict against an airline and an aircraft manufacturer for the death of a 36-year-old scientist arising from a major commercial airliner accident. The verdict was rendered in favor of his surviving wife and three children, one from a previous marriage. It was argued that the deceased would have been earning $112,000 annually by the time of trial and would have received raises of at least 10 percent per year and a large pension. The verdict was awarded by a jury in a large West Coast city.

➤ A $48,000 verdict in favor of a four-year-old child who suffered a four-inch laceration on her arm, resulting in $3,000 in medical bills, a permanent two-inch scar and loss of sensation. The injury was caused by a "pinch point" on a children's backyard swing set. The verdict was rendered by a jury in a suburban county near a large East Coast city.

Joint and Several Liability

One of the basic concepts of American law is the rule of *joint and several liability*. This phrase means, simply, that each person who contributes to an injury is responsible for the entire sum awarded as damages. Even when several people have contributed to the plaintiff's injury, the plaintiff can recover the entire award from any one of them. The rule of joint and several liability is sometimes called the "deep pocket" rule, because it encourages the plaintiff to find a defendant with adequate financial resources or insurance—deep pockets full of money—who can be shown to have some small share of the fault for the injury.

Perhaps more than any other factor, the rule of joint and several liability has been responsible for the proliferation of product liability lawsuits. Under this rule, a plaintiff who can show that a manufacturer had some responsibility for his injuries may recover the *entire* damage award from that manufacturer, even if its responsibility was small compared to that of others. This rule is a great benefit to the plaintiff because the manufacturer is often the only party potentially responsible for the plaintiff's injury who has any significant financial resources or who is not immune from liability.

If a court requires such a manufacturer to pay the entire amount of a judgment, the manufacturer may have a remedy against other parties who share responsibility for the accident. This remedy is called *contribution*. It is useful only if the other parties have resources to satisfy the award, are not immune from suit and have not already settled with the plaintiff.

The following example illustrates the burden the rule of joint and several liability places on the manufacturer. An automobile driver is injured in a collision with another automobile. The jury finds the injured driver 20 percent responsible for the accident, the other driver 75 percent responsible and the manufacturer of one of the vehicles 5 percent responsible. In that situation, the injured driver may, in most states, collect 80 percent of his damages from the manufacturer, even though the plaintiff was four times as responsible for his injuries. The manufacturer is left with a claim for contribution against the driver of the other car, who may have no resources to satisfy that claim. In some states the 20 percent responsibility attributed to the injured driver does not reduce his strict liability claim against the manufacturer. In those states, the injured driver may then recover 100 percent of his total damages from the manufacturer, who was only 5 percent responsible for the accident.

On-the-job injuries are another common situation where the joint and several liability rule encourages lawsuits against manufacturers. Workers' compensation laws generally prohibit an employee from suing his employer or fellow employees for on-the-job injuries. In lieu of the right to sue the employer, the employee has the right to a guaranteed payment in the event of a workplace accident. Often these workers' compensation payments are small in relation to the amount of damages that could be recovered in a lawsuit.

While workers' compensation laws prohibit injured employees from suing employers and fellow employees, suits against all other persons responsible for the injury are allowed. Accordingly, injured workers frequently bring product liability suits against the manufacturers of products involved in their injuries to supplement the amount received from workers' compensation. Under the rule of joint and several liability, a manufacturer that is 10 percent responsible for a worker's injuries will have to pay 100 percent of the damage award even though the employer was 90 percent responsible for failing to maintain the product or train its employees.

Immunity rules vary from state to state, but in most states the employer is immune from contribution suits in this situation. Indeed, the insurance company that pays the workers' compensation award usually has a lien on any employee recoveries from other parties. Consequently, the manufacturer ends up reimbursing the employer's insurer for injuries that were mostly the employer's fault. In a few states employers are not immune from contribution lawsuits even though they are immune from suit directly by the injured employees.

Product manufacturers and other target defendants (e.g., governmental entities), along with their insurers, have sought to have this unfair rule of joint and several liability abolished or modified by statute. Some of those efforts have succeeded, and in a few states the rule has been totally abolished. In still others, the rule has been modified or abolished when the plaintiff's own conduct contributed substantially to causing the accident. In California, a voters' initiative abolished joint and several liability for noneconomic damages.

Conflicting State Laws

The manufacture, sale and use of products often involve activities that take place in a number of different states, each with its own product liability law. A court hearing a lawsuit over such a product must choose a rule of law from the rules of the involved states. These laws may differ or even contradict each other.

For example, a car with defective brakes manufactured in Michigan and sold by a dealer in Connecticut hits a careless pedestrian from New Jersey when the driver is unable to stop the car on a street in New York. Each of these states may have different legal rules that apply to the various issues involved in a subsequent product liability suit. If the pedestrian's injuries were caused in part by his own carelessness, one state's rule might bar the claim, another's might allow full recovery and a third's might reduce the recovery by the pedestrian's proportionate share of the fault. Obviously, the outcome of the lawsuit will be greatly influenced by the choice of applicable law.

Each state has its own rules for choosing which state's law to apply in this kind of situation. In the past most states applied the law of the place where the injury occurred; in our example, the law of New York, where the accident took place, would have been applied even though it might be a place with little other connection to the parties or the product.

More recently, most states have adopted new rules that apply the law of the state with most connection with the parties and the strongest interest in determining a particular issue in the lawsuit. That state is frequently said to be the one with "the most significant relation-ship" to the occurrence and the parties. The purpose of these new rules is to apply the law of the state whose policies and interests would be advanced by the application of its law. Conversely, the new rules seek to avoid the application of the law of a state whose policies and interests either are irrelevant to the occurrence or would be thwarted by the application of its law. These rules may permit the application of the laws of different states to different issues in the same lawsuit.

These new choice-of-law rules give the court broader discretion in deciding which state's law to apply, and the court's decision is often difficult to predict. States likely to have an interest in an occurrence leading to a product liability lawsuit include *(a)* the state where the injury occurred; *(b)* the state where the conduct causing the injury occurred; *(c)* the state(s) where the parties have their domicile, residence, nationality, place of incorporation and place of business; and *(d)* the state where the relationship, if any, between the parties is centered.

In our example, it is difficult to select one state as having the most significant relationship to the occurrence and the parties. To apply the new rules, a court would first determine the relevant laws and interests of the involved states. Assume that Michigan, where the car was manufactured, and New Jersey, where the pedestrian lives, both have comparative negligence laws that would reduce the pedestrian's recovery in strict liability by his proportionate share of fault. Assume further that the law of New York, where the accident occurred, does not reduce the recovery of a strict liability claimant for his own negligence.

The purpose of New York's law is to ensure full compensation for injuries. But because the pedestrian lives in New Jersey, New York will not be affected by the degree of compensation paid to him and really has no significant interest in the application of its law to this case.

Conversely, Michigan and New Jersey, respectively, are home to the manufacturer, who will pay for the injuries, and the pedestrian, who will be paid. These states have the greatest interest in the degree of recovery allowed. Michigan is interested in the continued financial well-being of its resident manufacturer. New Jersey is interested that its resident recover enough so as not to be a burden on the state's resources. Moreover, Michigan and New Jersey are interested in deterring both careless pedestrians and the manufacture of defective automobiles, a result that can be achieved by application of comparative-fault principles. In this case, then, a court would probably apply the rule of law followed by Michigan and New Jersey, even though the accident occurred in New York.

If this case involved a manufacturer from a foreign country, the same type of choice-of-law analysis would be applied, but the judge is likely to experience greater difficulty determining the laws and interests of a foreign country as opposed to another state within the United States.

Modern choice-of-law rules have added an element of uncertainty to product liability lawsuits. And their application generally has not been kind to manufacturers. In many cases, the court chooses the law that enhances the plaintiff's recovery.

THE
PRODUCT LIABILITY
LAWSUIT

➤ 2 ◄

In American courts, product liability lawsuits proceed in essentially the same manner as other types of lawsuits. Although the various state and federal courts each have their own unique rules of procedure, the rules have much in common, and the typical steps in a product liability lawsuit can be described.

Initiation of the Lawsuit

A lawsuit typically begins when the plaintiff files a document called a *complaint* in the court where he has chosen to sue. The complaint names all parties seeking recovery (the *plaintiffs*) and all parties from whom they seek recovery (the *defendants*). The complaint also contains a brief statement explaining the claim. In a product liability case, this statement will include the date, location and nature of the accident; the injuries alleged; and the product involved. The complaint usually states a defendant's relationship to the product (such as manufacturer or seller) and identifies the legal theories by which the plaintiff seeks to establish liability (strict liability, negligence or breach of warranty). The complaint may, but need not, state the sum of money the plaintiff seeks to recover.

In addition to filing the complaint with the court, the plaintiff must also arrange for the complaint to be formally presented to each defendant, together with a *summons* with instructions to the defendant. This formal presentation is called *service* of the summons and complaint. In many jurisdictions all that is required to serve a summons and complaint is that they be mailed to the defendant. When the defendant is a foreign citizen, international treaties may control the method of service. Filing and service of the complaint set the legal process in motion.

Most product liability lawsuits are brought by a single plaintiff. However, some product-related accidents result in injuries to more than one person, and in such a situation the injured parties can join together, hire one lawyer and file a single lawsuit. In some limited instances, one plaintiff may be allowed to represent other similarly situated persons in what is called a *class action*.

Location of the Lawsuit

Federal and State Courts Each state has its own system of courts in which product liability suits may be brought. The procedures followed by these courts are governed by the state's own rules. The federal government also administers a system of courts. These federal courts are located in every state, but they all operate under the same federal procedures. In addition, each federal court has local rules governing its own procedures.

Most state trial courts are authorized to decide all types of cases, including product liability cases. Federal courts, however, cannot hear a product liability case unless the lawsuit falls within one of the recognized bases for federal *subject matter jurisdiction*.

This means that most product liability claims in federal court are based on a statute that gives the court jurisdiction to hear disputes between a plaintiff from one state and a defendant from a different state or from a foreign country, as long as the value of the plaintiff's claims exceeds $50,000. Jurisdiction under this statute is called *diversity jurisdiction* because there is diversity of citizenship between the plaintiff and the defendant.

In the exercise of its diversity jurisdiction, a federal court may decide, for instance, a claim for $100,000 brought by an injured New York citizen against a Japanese automobile manufacturer, a California automobile distributor and an Oregon automobile retailer. If the injured plaintiff lived in Oregon there would be no diversity jurisdiction over the claim because the plaintiff would be from the same state as one of the defendants. The plaintiff would not be able to bring a case in federal court unless he decided not to sue the Oregon defendant. When a federal court hears a matter within its diversity jurisdiction, it generally applies state law to the substantive legal issues in the case, although it applies its own procedural rules.

If a case brought in state court could have been brought in federal court because of diversity of citizenship, the defendants—if they act promptly—can usually have the case transferred to federal court. This transfer is called *removal*. Whether removal is a good idea in a particular case depends on many considerations of trial and pretrial strategy.

In addition to claims within the federal court's diversity jurisdiction, there is one other type of product liability claim commonly asserted in federal courts, namely, a claim within the federal court's *admiralty jurisdiction*. Generally, the federal courts have jurisdiction concurrent with the state courts over product liability claims arising out of accidents that occur on navigable waters when the alleged wrong bears a significant relationship to traditional maritime activity. When a claim is within the admiralty jurisdiction of the federal court, federal law applies to all issues presented by that claim. In recent years the federal courts have fashioned a body of product liability law very similar to the law followed in the majority of states.

Personal Jurisdiction, Venue and Inconvenient Forum   The plaintiff decides the state in which the action will be brought and whether it will be filed in state or federal court. It is then up to the defendant to decide whether to contest the plaintiff's choice. There are several grounds for such a contest.

The first possible argument is that the court lacks *personal jurisdiction* over the defendant. A court does not have the power to decide the legal rights and responsibilities of defendants who are not residents of that state and who have not engaged in purposeful activities in that state. Only defendants who have maintained some minimum level of connection with the forum state and have benefited from the protections of the state's laws may reasonably be called on to defend against claims filed in that state. The United States Constitution protects defendants, be they individuals or companies, from having to defend claims brought in a distant or inconvenient forum with which they have no substantial relationship.

The United States Supreme Court has said that to satisfy the constitutional test, a defendant must have "minimum contacts" with the forum state, so that forcing it to defend itself in that state does not offend "traditional notions of fair play and substantial justice." Lower courts have disagreed about what kinds of activities by a manufacturer will be considered sufficient to establish minimum contacts. Some courts have held that a manufacturer who is aware that the final product is being marketed in the forum state cannot claim to be surprised when it is sued in that state. For example, personal jurisdiction was exercised over a Japanese automobile manufacturer that sold completed vehicles to an American corporation in Tokyo. The manufacturer had no contacts with any of our states, but the American corporation sold those vehicles throughout the United States. The court held that the manufacturer's sales to the American corporation, its efforts to put the vehicles into the "stream of commerce" and its encouragement of those sales and revenue all evidenced its affirmative intent that the vehicles reach the individual states; therefore, it must reasonably anticipate being sued in a state where one of its vehicles causes injury.

Besides the constitutional limitations on a court's personal jurisdiction, most states have passed laws that list the kinds of contacts a nonresident defendant must have with the state before its courts will exercise personal jurisdiction. Common examples of these contacts are as follows: transacting any business in the state directly or by agent; regularly doing or soliciting business in the state; owning, using or possessing real estate within the state; and causing an injury by an act or omission within the state. Personal jurisdiction is a defense that a foreign manufacturer should always consider asserting when sued, particularly when the plaintiff has selected a forum that is not the defendant's place of operation or the place where the plaintiff's injury occurred.

In addition to the requirement of personal jurisdiction, state and federal statutes frequently place other limitations on where actions can be brought. These statutes dictate the proper place, or *venue*, for a lawsuit, embodying rules designed to ensure that lawsuits proceed in a forum reasonably related to the parties or their dispute. Typical venue provisions permit suit to be brought where the plaintiff resides, where all the defendants reside or are licensed to do business or where the incident giving rise to the lawsuit occurred.

Although a plaintiff generally has the right to bring a lawsuit before any court that has proper jurisdiction and venue, the court may dismiss the action if trial in the chosen forum would be unduly burdensome for the court and the parties. This is called a *forum non conveniens dismissal.* A court will dismiss for forum non conveniens only when there is another, more convenient court available to the plaintiff, either in the United States or a foreign country. If the lawsuit is in a federal court and the court determines that the lawsuit could more conveniently be heard in the federal court of a different state, it may simply transfer the action. Otherwise, the usual remedy is to dismiss the action and give the plaintiff an opportunity to refile the claim in the more convenient forum.

The forum non conveniens doctrine focuses on the convenience of the parties, the witnesses and the court. The action will be retained in the forum chosen by the plaintiff unless the defendant can make a strong showing that trial in that forum would be unduly burdensome. If the court dismisses the action on forum non conveniens grounds, it may require the defendant to submit to certain conditions, such as a waiver of any applicable statute of limitations in the alternative forum or an agreement not to contest personal jurisdiction in the alternative forum. Forum non conveniens dismissals are most commonly granted in suits brought by foreign plaintiffs for injuries that occurred outside the United States. In such cases, much of the necessary evidence is located in a foreign country, making litigation in the United States inconvenient to the court, the witnesses and the parties.

Defendant's Answer to Plaintiff's Complaint

The complaint that a plaintiff serves and files to commence a lawsuit has already been described. As noted, its purpose is to identify the plaintiff and the defendants and to notify the defendants of the basis of the plaintiff's claims against them.

When the complaint is served, it is accompanied by a document called a *summons.* The summons contains instructions to the defendant about how it must respond to the complaint. The defendant has a certain amount of time (usually 20 to 60 days) within which it is required to respond to the complaint. In most courts a defendant can respond to the complaint with either an *answer* or a *motion to dismiss* the complaint. Either response must be filed with the court and a copy delivered to the plaintiff.

If the plaintiff properly serves the defendant and the defendant does not respond within the required time period, the plaintiff can attempt to obtain a *default judgment* against the defendant. Under this procedure, the plaintiff asks the court to grant judgment against the defendant in the amount requested because the defendant has not responded in the required time and, therefore, has not contested the plaintiff's allegations. Because of the availability of default, it is important that a defendant served with a summons and complaint act quickly to respond. The best way to see that this happens is to develop procedures in advance for handling lawsuit papers so that they are transmitted immediately to the proper person within the company, and then to the company's insurer and/or lawyers.

The answer filed by a defendant is a formal statement of the defendant's position and requires no action by the court. In its answer, the defendant must respond point by point to the allegations in the plaintiff's complaint, admitting any allegations it knows to be true (or, through reasonable inquiry, could determine to be true) and denying those it believes to be false. If the defendant cannot determine the truth of an allegation because of insufficient information, it can so indicate (after having made a reasonable inquiry into the facts) and, on this basis, deny the allegation.

The answer should then set forth any affirmative defenses the defendant may have. As discussed in Chapter I, an affirmative defense is a legal basis for avoiding or reducing the defendant's liability. Examples of affirmative defenses include these:

➤ *The plaintiff's own fault caused or contributed to the accident, thus barring or reducing the plaintiff's recovery from the defendant.*

➤ *The case was filed after the time limit set forth in the applicable statute of limitations has expired.*

➤ *The court lacks jurisdiction over the action or the defendant.*

➤ *Service of the summons on the defendant was not made properly.*

➤ *The same claim has already been litigated and resolved between the same parties in a past proceeding (a defense called* res judicata).

➤ *The contract between the plaintiff and the defendant contains a provision which limits or disclaims liability.*

There are many other affirmative defenses a defendant might assert in response to a plaintiff's complaint.

As an alternative to filing an answer, the defendant can file a motion to dismiss the complaint. A motion to dismiss is a way to raise a defense easily presented, such as lack of jurisdiction, at the outset of the lawsuit. In the federal courts, every defense that can be raised by a motion can also be inserted in the answer and brought to the court for resolution at a later time. In some states, though, certain defenses—typically lack of personal jurisdiction over the defendant—must be raised by a motion prior to filing the answer, or those defenses are waived.

In its answer, the defendant can also assert claims against other parties to the litigation. Such claims when asserted against the plaintiff are called *counterclaims* and when asserted against a codefendant are called *cross-claims*. For example, an automobile manufacturer, when sued by a driver and a passenger in a single lawsuit, may assert a counterclaim against the driver stating that if the manufacturer is liable to the passenger, the driver is in turn liable to the manufacturer for all or part of the passenger's damages. A claim by a defendant against a person or company who is neither a plaintiff nor a codefendant in the lawsuit is called a *third-party claim,* and the person against whom the claim is asserted is called a *third-party defendant.*

Whether to assert a cross-claim against a codefendant or name a third-party defendant is a matter of strategy. Certainly, when the other party is the manufacturer's own component supplier, the manufacturer will want to consider whether the assertion of such a claim has the effect of making it appear that there is more substance to the plaintiff's claim than there really is. There is also the risk that two defendants attempting to establish each other's liability will help the plaintiff establish his case more easily. If the plaintiff has neglected through oversight to name a third party, the defendant may want to bring the identity of that third party to the plaintiff's attention before the statute of limitations expires on the plaintiff's direct claim. If the plaintiff elects not to sue the third party directly, the defendant may need to file a third-party complaint before the statute of limitations expires.

Pretrial Discovery

After the complaint is filed, and generally after all answers are filed, the lawsuit proceeds to what is usually called the *discovery* phase. During this phase, each party attempts to discover facts, identify witnesses and obtain documents that support its position in the dispute; it may also learn about the opponent's case and weaknesses in its own case. Court rules typically provide several methods for each party to get information from other parties in the lawsuit and from nonparties. The purpose of these rules is to allow the parties to gather all the relevant facts before trial begins. When evidence is located outside the United States, international treaties may control.

Interrogatories Usually one party asks another party written questions called *interrogatories*. A plaintiff typically asks manufacturers questions about the design or manufacture of the product involved, warnings provided with the product, how the product works, the identities of employees knowledgeable about the product, the existence and contents of documents relevant to the product, the defendant's knowledge of the accident and whether the product has been involved in any similar accidents. Typical questions posed by the defendant to the plaintiff include inquiries about the manner in which the accident occurred, the identities of eyewitnesses, the facts on which the plaintiff bases his theories of liability against the defendant, the extent of the plaintiff's actual injuries and the amount of money lost by the plaintiff because of his injuries (this will involve questions about past income, projected future income and dependent family members).

A party served with interrogatories must answer them in writing and under oath within a certain amount of time (usually 20 to 30 days) or object to the questions if there is a valid reason not to answer them. In practice, the parties frequently take longer to answer. Often lawyers develop very extensive "form" interrogatories, sometimes including dozens of complex questions. Answering these form questions can impose a large burden, and as a result many courts now limit the number of interrogatories that a party can ask.

Because answers to interrogatories are almost invariably written or edited by lawyers, they are not particularly useful for obtaining candid, spontaneous answers to difficult questions. On the other hand, they can be an inexpensive way to get background information.

Some questions, such as those that call for the collective knowledge of a corporate party, can be more effectively asked by interrogatory than by questions posed to individual witnesses.

Requests for Production of Documents and Things   Discovery rules permit each party to request and inspect documents and other tangible items from other parties. These *document requests* are submitted in writing. Like answers to interrogatories, requested documents must be produced for inspection within a specific amount of time after a party receives the request (usually 20 to 30 days). Examples of documents a product liability plaintiff typically requests from a defendant include investigative reports on the accident, design or manufacturing drawings and specifications, notes or minutes from meetings and reports of similar accidents or prior problems with the product. Examples of documents generally requested from the plaintiff are photographs or other documents concerning the accident, income tax statements to verify income and any other documents supporting the plaintiff's contentions. The definition of "document" is broad. It encompasses just about any tangible thing, including personal notes, desk diaries, appointment calendars, photographs, tape recordings and data stored by computer. The rule that permits production of documents also permits parties to examine tangible items, such as the allegedly defective product.

Many companies are astonished at the extent to which they can be required to open their engineering and service files for inspection by a plaintiff's lawyer. But this is a fact of life, and, as discussed in Chapter III, the best way for a company to deal with it is to educate its personnel to be conscious of the potential implications of what they write.

Physical and Mental Examinations   Discovery rules also permit examination of a party whose physical or mental condition is at issue in a lawsuit. The most common use of this rule in a product liability action is to have a physician who has been selected by the defendant examine the plaintiff to determine the actual extent of the plaintiff's injuries. The only disadvantage is that any report written as a result of the examination must be made available to the plaintiff.

Requests for Admissions   Any party may serve another party with written requests to admit particular allegations. The party on whom such requests are served must admit or deny the allegations or state why the allegations cannot be admitted or denied. If that party fails to answer within the time required by court rules (usually 20 to 30 days), it will be deemed to have admitted the requests. These admissions will bind the party during the rest of the lawsuit. If a party unreasonably refuses to admit an allegation, it can later be charged the cost the requesting party incurred in proving it.

In most circumstances, requests for admission are not particularly useful because courts are often reluctant to punish a party's unreasonable refusal to admit an obviously true fact. On the other hand, if the other party does admit a request for admission, that response is more binding than either an interrogatory answer or deposition testimony, because many courts will not allow a party to contradict an earlier response to a request to admit.

Depositions   Any party may demand that another party to the lawsuit or any other person appear for a *deposition*. A deposition is a proceeding in which the person requested to appear (the *deponent*) can be asked questions under oath by attorneys for any of the parties. The questions and answers are recorded by a stenographer, who makes a verbatim transcript of the proceeding. Some depositions are also videotaped. The videotape or the typed transcript may be used at trial if the deponent is unavailable. They also may be used at trial to discredit a deponent if his trial testimony conflicts with his prior deposition testimony. Finally, the deposition testimony of a party or an employee of a party can be used to establish any fact stated in the deposition that is adverse to the party's interest at trial.

The plaintiff will typically take the depositions of people familiar with the design, testing or manufacture of the product or who investigated the accident or similar accidents. The plaintiff can obtain the names of these employees from the defendant's answers to interrogatories or from the documents produced. Or the plaintiff can simply ask the defendant to designate an employee who can testify about a particular subject matter.

The defendant will typically take the depositions of the plaintiff and any eyewitnesses to the injury. The defendant will also depose people with whom the plaintiff has consulted and plans to use at trial to support his claim that the product was defective or to substantiate the extent of his injuries or damages. These people are generally referred to as *expert witnesses* because they claim particular expertise in some field relevant to the issues in the lawsuit. For example, the plaintiff could hire an engineer as an expert witness on the design of the product, a doctor as an expert witness on the plaintiff's injuries or an economist as an expert witness on the income lost by the plaintiff. The defendant may also hire an expert witness to defend the design of the product or an economist to dispute the plaintiff's damages. All parties generally depose the other parties' experts prior to trial.

Objections to Discovery Under the discovery rules, parties may seek information about any matter either directly relevant to the subject matter of the lawsuit or reasonably likely to lead to the discovery of relevant information, unless the information is privileged. If the discovery request seeks irrelevant or privileged material, the party from whom discovery is sought may respond by objecting rather than by answering.

The most common *privileges* invoked in discovery objections are for attorney-client communications and attorneys' work product. Most communications between a party and his lawyer are privileged and need not be disclosed during discovery or trial. This attorney-client privilege is designed to encourage full and frank client disclosures by securing a cloak of confidentiality for these communications. The work-product privilege protects from disclosure the preparation done by or for a lawyer in anticipation of litigation. However, this protection is incomplete because disclosure may be required by the court upon a showing of substantial need.

Objections may also be made to the form of discovery requests. For example, it is common to object to discovery requests that are unduly burdensome, vague or confusing. These types of discovery requests can be clarified and narrowed through negotiations between the parties' lawyers.

Protective Orders American discovery rules are abused frequently. It is easy for a lawyer to describe by category and ask for what may turn out to be hundreds of thousands of documents. When the plaintiff's counsel attempts such abuse, the defendant should certainly object to the discovery request and may also want to consider seeking a *protective order*. Protective orders may be sought when the plaintiff's discovery request seeks patently irrelevant information or when the plaintiff tries to make discovery as expensive as possible for the defendant to obtain an attractive settlement. Protective orders can also prevent the disclosure of proprietary information, trade secrets or sensitive data.

Orders to Compel Discovery and Sanctions   If a party fails to respond to discovery requests adequately, the requesting party may ask the court for appropriate relief. If the court agrees that an adequate response to a discovery request has not been made, it may order compliance with the request and impose a variety of sanctions. Some of the sanctions allowed include deeming certain contested facts to have been admitted by the sanctioned party and requiring that party to pay the expenses (including attorneys' fees) incurred by the opposing party in obtaining the order to comply. For extreme discovery violations, the court may enter judgment against the sanctioned party.

In other words, a manufacturer could lose a lawsuit for failure to comply with a discovery request. It is obviously important to take discovery requests very seriously. One example of a manufacturer's refusal to produce documents resulted in entry of a judgment of liability, in a case involving a plaintiff who had been severely burned while wearing a garment produced by the manufacturer. The plaintiff had requested copies of all complaints and communications concerning injuries or deaths allegedly caused by the burning of nightwear manufactured or marketed by the defendant, a very large American company. The defendant failed to make a timely objection to the discovery request. It later offered as its only justification for not complying the fact that it indexed claims alphabetically by claimant rather than by product or type of injury. The court rejected this justification, noting that a defendant may not avoid production by using a system of recordkeeping that conceals rather than discloses relevant records. The court felt entry of a default judgment was appropriate, given what it perceived to be the defendant's pattern of continuous, flagrant and willful violation of the discovery rules.

Summary Judgment

In most jurisdictions, if the facts needed to resolve the parties' entire dispute (or any distinct portion of it) are established or cannot reasonably be contested, the judge can make a decision without a trial. In such an instance, the judge applies the law to the undisputed facts. In most courts this procedure is called a *summary judgment.*

A summary judgment resolving an entire case is generally more likely for the defendant than for the plaintiff in a product liability case. It is rare for a court to grant summary judgment on issues like the existence or nonexistence of negligence or a product defect. On the other hand, a defendant will sometimes have a defense appropriate for disposition by summary judgment, such as statute of limitations or contractual disclaimer. The issue of causation is also sometimes appropriate for disposition by summary judgment.

The attitude of trial judges toward summary judgment varies from place to place. Historically, many courts took a very cautious attitude toward summary judgment, but this attitude is softening as trial courts look for ways to ease their congested dockets. Because of the historic reluctance of many courts to use the summary judgment device, defense attorneys are sometimes unwilling to go to the expense of filing such a motion. This is often a mistake. Most summary judgment motions are denied because the party making the motion failed to demonstrate to the court that there really was no factual dispute or that proof of some essential element of the plaintiff's case did not exist. In other words, most summary judgment motions lose because they are not well-conceived and well-prepared. A carefully planned motion may succeed, especially if the plaintiff overconfidently responds with a hurried, poorly written opposition. In any case, as long as the motion is not frivolous, it is frequently useful to file a summary judgment motion where the defense is strong, just to indicate to the plaintiff and the judge the strength of the defendant's case. It is not unusual for a plaintiff facing a strong summary judgment motion to settle the claim on a reasonable basis or even to surrender completely.

Bifurcation and Consolidation

Normally, a single lawsuit results in a single trial. There are exceptions. A single lawsuit may result in certain claims or issues being tried separately. This is called *bifurcation.* Separate trials on liability and damages are the most common bifurcation, although in most jurisdictions the court may order separate trials on any issue or group of issues that can conveniently be tried separately. Whether the same jury will be used for the separate trials is decided by the trial court, as is whether to hold the trials one right after another or to allow a lapse of time between them.

Conversely, separate lawsuits pending in the same court may be *consolidated* for certain purposes, including trial. Sometimes several suits may be consolidated for a single trial on liability, followed by separate trials on each party's damages claim, should liability be found.

Whether a product liability defendant should seek either consolidation or bifurcation is a question of strategy that depends on the facts of the particular case. The following rules of thumb may be useful:

➤ *Consolidation of several cases for pretrial proceedings is generally useful for the defendant if different lawyers are involved for various plaintiffs, because most courts will require the plaintiffs to coordinate pretrial discovery, which reduces the defendant's burden.*

➤ *Consolidation of several cases for trial is generally in the defendant's interest if all claims arise out of the same occurrence. If the cases are consolidated for one liability trial, all plaintiffs are bound by the outcome. On the other hand, if the cases are not consolidated, the rule in most jurisdictions (unfair as this may sound) is that while none of the other plaintiffs is bound by a decision adverse to the first plaintiff, the defendant may be bound in all other cases by the outcome of the first-tried case if it is adverse to the defendant.*

➤ *Consolidation of several cases for trial should generally be avoided if the claims arise out of separate accidents. A single trial of such claims will present to the jury the fact that the product was involved in multiple accidents, which is likely to prejudice the defense.*

➤ *Separate trials of liability and damages work to the advantage of defendants in most cases. Bifurcation can be particularly beneficial to the defendant if the plaintiff's liability case is weak and the injuries are severe. On the other hand, there may be times when a defendant will want the jury hearing the liability evidence to hear the damage evidence as well, especially if the plaintiff appears to be a malingerer or the damage claim is obviously exaggerated.*

Trial

The purpose of a trial is to resolve the factual and legal disputes between the parties. Although trial procedures vary among jurisdictions, the basic features are the same.

Judge and Jury   One aspect of the American judicial system that evokes substantial curiosity on the part of foreign manufacturers is the *jury* system.   In virtually all product liability cases (the only significant exception being cases within the admiralty jurisdiction of the federal courts), the parties are entitled to have the matter determined by a jury.

Juries in product liability cases usually consist of either six or twelve people.   In federal court, the jury is usually six people, whose decision on all issues must be unanimous.   Most states use twelve-person juries, but unanimity is generally not required.   In most courts, one of the parties must file a timely *jury demand*, or the right to a jury trial will be waived.   In the federal courts, a jury must be demanded in the very early stages of the proceedings.   The plaintiff typically includes a jury demand in the complaint.   If the plaintiff does not demand a jury trial, the defendant can.

Whether a manufacturer is better off trying the case before a judge or before a jury is in each case a judgment to be based on such factors as who the assigned judge is, the likely composition of the jury and whether there are aspects of the case that are likely to arouse strong emotions.

In a trial without a jury (called a *bench trial*), the judge makes all legal rulings governing trial procedures and also decides the factual disputes at issue in the action.   In a jury trial, the judge presides over the trial and makes all legal rulings, but the jury decides the factual issues.   Except for the obvious difference that in a bench trial there is no jury selection, jury instructions nor jury deliberation, the trial format is generally the same for both bench trials and jury trials.

Jury Selection   The first step in a jury trial is to select the jury members.   A panel of prospective jurors randomly selected from the community is asked questions by the judge or the lawyers or both.   This process is frequently referred to as *voir dire*.   Its purpose is to ascertain the jurors' backgrounds, possible biases and prejudices and other information designed to determine their impartiality concerning the issues in the lawsuit. Prospective jurors whose answers indicate that they could not be impartial are dismissed from the panel. A request by a lawyer to dismiss a juror on such a basis is known as a *challenge for cause.* In addition, many judges are willing to dismiss people whose jobs or personal circumstances make long jury service difficult. As a result, juries frequently have a disproportionate number of unemployed and retired persons and homemakers, although in some places there is a trend toward requiring jury service from all citizens.

In addition to dismissals for cause, the lawyers for each side may remove a specified number of prospective jurors from the jury panel without giving any explanation whatsoever. These are known as *peremptory challenges.* Each side is typically permitted three peremptory challenges.

The people not dismissed for cause or peremptorily are then empaneled as the jury. In long cases, the court may also empanel a number of alternate jurors, who attend and watch the trial just as the regular jurors do. If a member of the regular jury becomes ill or cannot complete jury service for other reasons, an alternate can then substitute for him. Unless such a substitution occurs, the alternates are excused at the end of the trial and do not participate in the jury's deliberations and decisions.

Opening Statements The trial begins with the presentation of *opening statements.* Opening statements give the jury and the judge a preview of the evidence to be presented during trial. They are supposed to be factual and not argumentative. The plaintiff makes the first opening statement. The defendant may make an opening statement immediately after the plaintiff is finished or wait until all of the plaintiff's evidence has been presented. Ordinarily the defendant will make its opening statement before the plaintiff's evidence is presented, but if there is more than one defendant with similar interests, it can be effective for one defendant to wait until the plaintiff's case has been completed.

Presentation of Evidence After opening statements, the plaintiff presents his evidence first. The plaintiff has the *burden of proof,* which means that he must convince the jury that the preponderance of the evidence favors his position. Evidence can be presented through the testimony of witnesses and the use of physical exhibits such as documents. It can also be presented through the deposition testimony of unavailable witnesses and through stipulations of undisputed facts, which are simply read aloud in court.

Evidence of a witness is introduced by answers to questions. The lawyer calling the witness asks questions, which the witness then answers. This is known as *direct examination*. Following direct examination, the opposing party's lawyer may *cross-examine* the witness. This is an opportunity to undermine the witness's testimony by asking further questions about the subjects covered during direct examination. The cross-examining attorney may also ask questions designed to show the witness's bias or lack of knowledge. In many jurisdictions, the judge may ask the witness questions. Jurors are not allowed to ask questions, but a few judges allow them to write out suggested questions for the judge to ask.

During witness examination, the lawyer not asking questions may *object* to any improper question. The judge rules then on whether the question should be answered. That ruling depends on whether the question calls for an answer that will be admissible evidence. For example, hearsay may not be admissible. Of course, a lawyer may not wish to object to inadmissible evidence when it is helpful to his client. A lawyer may also object to the introduction of improper exhibits.

After presenting all of his evidence, the plaintiff *rests* his case. At this time, the defendant may ask the judge for a *directed verdict* if the plaintiff has failed to introduce sufficient evidence for the jury to find against the defendant. Such requests are seldom granted. The judge usually reserves his decision or finds that the plaintiff has presented enough evidence, and the trial proceeds.

The defendant then presents its evidence. If there are multiple defendants, they present their cases in an agreed order. The procedures for presentation of the defendants' cases are identical to those for the plaintiff's case, except that the defense lawyer conducts the direct examination and the other lawyers, including those of the codefendants, conduct the cross-examination.

Once all the evidence is in, the defense attorneys may again ask the judge for a directed verdict. If the judge believes that, based on the evidence, reasonable individuals could differ on the proper outcome of the case, the motion will be denied.

Closing Arguments   If the directed verdict motion is denied, the lawyers present *closing arguments.* During this phase each lawyer addresses the jury directly and summarizes the evidence, argues his interpretation of it and urges a finding in his client's favor. Normally, the plaintiff's closing argument is presented first, followed by arguments for each defendant. The plaintiff may then present a brief rebuttal argument. In some jurisdictions, the plaintiff argues only once, generally after the defendants.

Jury Instructions and Verdicts   After closing arguments, the judge gives the jurors instructions on the law. In a product liability case, they are given instructions on the applicable standards for manufacturer liability discussed in Chapter I. (A sample set of jury instructions is found in Appendix A.)

After hearing the judge's instructions, the jurors retire to a private jury room where they deliberate until they agree on a verdict. A verdict is simply a statement of the jury's findings of fact. There are two kinds of verdicts. A general verdict states the jury's overall conclusion, such as "The plaintiff has not proved his claim, and the defendant owes him nothing," or "The plaintiff has proved his claim and should recover $200,000 from the defendant."

In a *special verdict*, the jury answers specific questions submitted by the judge. These questions are usually proposed by the parties and ask about disputed factual issues. Some examples of questions that might be asked in a product liability case are as follows:

➤ *Did the defendant negligently design the product?*

➤ *Was the manufacture of the product defective?*

➤ *If both the plaintiff and the defendant were at fault in causing the plaintiff's injury, what percentage of fault is attributable to each?*

The questions should be devised so that the appropriate overall outcome of the case can be readily deduced from the answers.

The jury typically decides questions such as whether the product caused the accident or injury, whether the product was defective or unsafe and how much compensation, if any, the defendant should pay to the plaintiff. In product liability cases these questions often require the jury to evaluate highly technical testimony about product design, function and performance. The judge instructs the jury to decide these questions based solely on the evidence presented at trial and the legal standards explained by the judge. The jury is not required to explain the basis for its decision, and its discussions are held in private. The verdict, however, is announced in open court.

Jurisdictions differ over the number of jurors who must agree on the verdict. Some (including all federal courts) require a unanimous decision, while others permit agreement by a supermajority of jurors (usually 5 of 6 or 10 of 12). If the required number of jurors cannot agree on a verdict after a reasonable amount of time, the jury is dismissed and the case must be retried.

In a bench trial, the judge may either render a decision immediately or "take the case under advisement" and announce a decision at a later date. The court will frequently ask the parties for post-trial briefs, which summarize their contentions, before rendering a decision.

Appeal

If a party wishes to challenge a final judgment entered by a trial court, that party may appeal to an *appellate court*. An appellate court can either affirm the judgment of the trial court, reverse that judgment and send the case back to the trial court with instructions on how to proceed further or reverse the result reached in the trial court and enter a different judgment. An appellate court usually will reverse a judgment only if the trial court has made a significant error in its legal rulings or if there is essentially no evidence to support its decision. If the trial was free of material legal error, and if the appellate court believes that reasonable minds could reach different conclusions based on the factual evidence, it will affirm the judgment of the trial court, even though it might have reached a different result if it had made its own factual determinations.

Most states have two levels of appellate courts, an intermediate court of appeals and a supreme court. Appeals from trial courts in product liability cases are almost always directed initially to the intermediate appellate courts. The result reached by that court can usually be reviewed by the state's supreme court. In most states, an appeal to the supreme court will be considered only if that court agrees to hear the appeal. Generally, those courts accept only cases that will resolve unsettled issues of law or may change the law in a given area.

A judgment from a federal district court can be appealed to the federal court of appeals for the region in which the district court is located. A party can then ask that the decision of a federal appeals court be reviewed by the United States Supreme Court. The Supreme Court hears only a tiny number of the cases filed with it.

Where federal law is involved in a case tried in a state court, it is also possible to seek review of a state appellate decision in the United States Supreme Court. The Supreme Court rarely reviews state court decisions in product liability cases. Thus, the possibility of review by the United States Supreme Court is more theoretical than real.

Depending on the jurisdiction, an appeal can take from a few months to several years to resolve. Appeals are presented to the court through written petitions called *briefs*. The party appealing, known as the *appellant*, files the first brief. Responding parties, *appellees*, then file their briefs, which the appellant may answer with a reply brief. An *oral argument* for the case is usually then scheduled. At this argument, the lawyers argue their positions before a panel of appellate judges and answer any questions the judges ask. After oral argument, the judges confer and vote to determine the outcome. Once a majority of the panel agrees on an outcome, one of the judges writes an opinion explaining the panel's decision.

REDUCING
PRODUCT LIABILITY
EXPOSURE

➤ 3 ≺

There are many steps a manufacturer should consider taking to minimize its product liability exposure. Some of these reduce the likelihood of product liability claims by reducing the likelihood of product-related injuries occurring. Others improve your ability to defend your products, if an injury does occur, by limiting the plaintiff's ability to make distorted claims. Still other techniques deal with the handling of accidents, claims and lawsuits.

This chapter will discuss an approach to product liability prevention that integrates measures that can be taken at various steps of the process, from the earliest design phase of the product through trial of an actual claim. We should point out, however, that there are many ways to skin a cat and that manufacturers have varying approaches to their product liability problems. The suggestions made below may be useful for some manufacturers and not for others. At the very least they should stimulate thinking on the subject.

The Product Liability Prevention Manager

An important step you as a manufacturer can take to reduce your product liability exposure is to charge a specific manager with that responsibility and give him sufficient authority and independence to do the job. Ideally, for a large manufacturer, product liability prevention should be this person's only job, and he should report directly to senior management to assure that recommendations and concerns are not easily overruled or avoided by other managers.

Management should make it clear that this is an important job—not a "dead end" or a "final pasture." The ideal candidate would be a rising middle manager with a broad engineering background and exposure to other departments, such as sales and marketing, manufacturing and quality control, testing, customer service, publications, legal and insurance. It would be very useful if this manager had some legal training.

The product liability prevention manager should have direct responsibility for all of the preaccident and post-accident programs described below. He should also have direct involvement in any product liability litigation.

Preaccident Measures

Product Liability Education Programs If you are a product liability prevention manager, your most important responsibility is to alert your fellow employees to your company's product liability exposure, to make them sensitive to product liability concerns and to instruct them as to what they should and should not do. To be effective, this education program usually should be continuing and pervasive, reaching all employees in sensitive positions, including the highest levels of management.

There are a number of ways of reaching employees. Written materials, such as Chapters I and II of this primer, can be distributed to key personnel. Some manufacturers conduct periodic product liability lectures for their employees; attendance is mandatory. These lectures usually last about one hour, followed by a question period. Their primary purposes are to remind employees of the importance of product safety and reliability, point out potential problems and identify the types of employee conduct that can lead to trouble and make legal defense difficult. It is helpful to have these lectures presented by lawyers who have defended your company in product liability litigation and who can draw from actual experiences to illustrate their advice. These lectures are often of intense interest to the audience and generate questions from employees regarding specific matters on which they are working. These questions frequently reveal potential problem areas that can then be addressed by the product liability prevention program. These lectures should be repeated at least annually.

Written Records As product liability prevention manager, another responsibility you have is to make sure that your company creates and retains the kinds of records likely to be useful in defending your products in any litigation that may occur. Product liability claims frequently arise years after the product was designed and delivered. Knowledgeable personnel retire or change jobs, and memories fade. Thus, contemporaneous written records become a key element of proof in any product liability trial. You and your coworkers should retain the following types of documentation:

➢ *Records that describe each individual product's condition when it left the company;*

➢ *Records that show the product was properly inspected and tested and met industry or government standards;*

➢ *Records that show customers were given instructions regarding proper use of the product, warnings regarding hazards and notice of the availability of design options and improvements; and*

➢ *Records that contain disclaimer and indemnity agreements, both with suppliers and subcomponent manufacturers and with purchasers (i.e., records that will help you prove that legal responsibility for an injury should be borne by someone else).*

You should also recognize that some perfectly appropriate and valuable writings can be harmful if they are subject to being misused by a plaintiff's attorney to suggest a product was defective when in fact it was not. We cannot list all the different examples of such writings, but a few illustrations may be helpful.

Cost-benefit analyses
Writings that a skillful lawyer can argue suggest that it is cheaper to pay for injuries than to fix the product are extremely damaging. There have been cases in which manufacturers have expressly assigned monetary values to potential deaths and injuries and compared

those amounts with the cost of corrective action. Such cost-benefit analyses are not likely to sit well with a typical American jury.

Sometimes an employee creates writings of this nature quite innocently. A typical scenario might involve unverified and disputed claims that the product has injured several consumers. The employee writes a memo suggesting an improvement that could prevent such injuries. The suggestion is rejected because the expense is very great, and the actual improvement doubtful. Moreover, management doubts or at least is not convinced that any product defect exists at all. Subsequently, a consumer is injured and the plaintiff's lawyer uses the rejection of the employee suggestion ·to argue that the company willfully and wantonly gambled with the consumer's safety. Punitive damage awards arise from facts like these.

"CYA" memos

The term "cover your ass" and its acronym "CYA" are widely understood. Typically the memo writer wishes to create a record to show in advance that he is not responsible for some undesired event that either has occurred or may occur. For example, "I told those guys in manufacturing for weeks that the pinion gear would fail unless they increased the torque on the retaining nut." There may in fact be a real question whether the gear failed because of improper torque or because the consumer ran the machine above the red line. Once the plaintiff's lawyer has the CYA memo, he will have an easy time convincing the jury that torque is the problem.

Computer printouts of service difficulties

Most manufacturers receive feedback from consumers, distributors, agents and others about problems with their product. The feedback is frequently unverified and often wrong. For example, an automotive mechanic troubleshooting a rough-engine problem may replace the fuel control while in fact the problem lies in an intermittent short in the wiring harness. The fuel control replacement is reported to its manufacturer. A computer operator then enters it in the reliability records as a fuel control problem, where it gets lumped with all sorts of other fuel control problems—some real, others nonexistent. With enough of these, a plaintiff's lawyer can argue that the company's own records show that the product is unreliable.

Cryptic notes

After an airplane accident, an engineer at the home plant makes notes during his conversation with the company's on-the-scene investigator. The investigator says, "The airline believes a structural failure occurred because they see no evidence of a bomb." The engineer quickly jots down "structural failure—no bomb." Years later in litigation between a plaintiff (who insists there was a structural failure) and the manufacturer (which believes a bomb was involved), the cryptic note is turned over to the plaintiff's lawyer. The engineer who wrote the note is unavailable to explain it because he is—take your choice—dead, senile or disgruntled. At trial the plaintiff's lawyer reads the document (as often as possible) to the jury and argues, "Look what the airplane company was saying about the cause of the accident before they knew they were going to be sued."

Rough drafts

A service engineer writes a first draft of a recall letter suggesting that a product be modified by December of that year. For good reason, the effective date of the recall is changed in the final draft to July of the following year. The first draft languishes forgotten in the service engineer's desk—until it is produced for a plaintiff's lawyer whose client was injured in May. You can predict that the lawyer will argue that the service engineer got it right the first time and was overruled by managers willing to risk safety rather than deal with a tighter schedule.

Because court rules permit plaintiffs to gain access to documents of all kinds—reports, correspondence, memoranda, notes—your prevention program should apply to any type of tangible record, including data stored by computer. Employees' "personal work files" should also be included. Virtually every product liability defense lawyer has at least one story about an engineer who shows up to have his deposition taken with a personal file full of documents the lawyer has never seen before (and which he may have represented to opposing counsel did not exist).

As product liability prevention manager, you should educate employees to be sensitive to product liability implications whenever they write anything. It is obviously necessary, however, for employees to create new writings to make new products, improve old ones and solve problems. It is important not to chill that process with excessive concern over product liability exposure.

Employees should be advised: Write what you must write, but write with an appreciation that what you are writing may someday be read to a judge or jury by an unfriendly lawyer who may use it out of context or attempt to give it a meaning that you never intended. Normally, the closer the author sticks to the facts that he actually knows, the less chance there is of creating a harmful document. If necessary information is not known personally and its accuracy cannot be confirmed, then the author should describe the source of the information (e.g., "A customer reported that . . ."). Adherence to this guideline will ensure that at trial your company is not deemed to have admitted the accuracy of facts reported by a customer that turn out to have been incomplete or erroneous.

Some words have established, unfavorable meanings in product liability law. For example, the words "defect" and "failure" should be avoided if possible. Instead, the condition should be described factually. It is more precise, more accurate (and less legally dangerous) to say, "The product stopped operating when the connecting rod fractured," than to say, "The product failed because of a defect in the connecting rod."

If an employee writes a document that proposes an alternative course of action, such as a design change, and management decides not to follow the recommendation, a second document should be created to explain the reasons for that decision and complete the written record. This is commonly called "closing the loop." Many times the individual making the recommendation will not have had access to all relevant information when his recommendation was made and may himself close the loop by writing a second document acknowledging the wisdom of the final decision. If not, the decision maker should create the loop-closing document. Failure to close the loop on a proposed, unadopted design change can give a plaintiff's lawyer a valuable weapon. Your company will find it much easier to convince a jury that a written suggestion was unworkable when it has a contemporaneous (i.e., preaccident) loop-closing document explaining why the suggestion was not accepted.

Design, Instructions and Warnings   One of your jobs, as product liability prevention manager, may be to check that the engineers who design new products and product improvements and who write instructions and warnings do so in a manner that emphasizes product safety and reliability. The most important lesson here is that engineers anticipate the likely ways in which the product might be misused and then design, instruct and/or warn to eliminate or minimize hazards associated with such misuse.

When a new product is being developed, the manufacturer should have in mind the entire distribution chain for the product, the various types of uses and users of the product, and environments in which the product will be used. If the product is likely to be altered by someone in the distribution chain before it reaches the consumer or user, this possibility should be considered during product development. The skills, training and intelligence of the end-user should also be evaluated.

Early in the product development phase, it is a good idea to research and compile all potentially applicable government or industry regulations, standards and practices governing product design, manufacturing and instructions or warnings. Failure to comply with government regulations or to incorporate safety features used by your competitors may result in liability. Obviously, if you are unaware of applicable regulations, standards or practices, you are more likely to produce something not in compliance with them.

As the design progresses, you should try to predict the potential hazards that may arise during the product's use, including their likelihood of occurrence and the severity of consequences. This analysis should be done not only with respect to the intended uses of the product but also with respect to reasonably foreseeable misuses. Some manufacturers find it possible and useful to do failure mode and effect analyses (FMEAs). An FMEA will attempt to look at each way in which each product component could possibly fail during use and misuse, the probabilities of such a failure and the consequences or effect. The idea is to have a design that either eliminates the significant hazards from failures or makes the probability of failure remote so that such a failure is unlikely to occur during the life of the product.

The development of product instructions and warnings needs particular attention. Again, it will be helpful in avoiding product liability to consider not just the 95 percent of consumers who will use the product competently and safely, but also the 5 percent who will not.

Once you identify a hazard that should be warned against, you must write the text of the warning. Warnings should state not only how to use the product, but in many cases also how not to use it and the consequences of failing to heed the warning. If you fail to describe the consequences of product misuse, an injured consumer can claim that he did not under-stand the seriousness of the risk created by his conduct. For example, incredible as it sounds, some silver-tongued plaintiff's lawyer may be able to convince a jury that it is not enough merely to tell the user not to operate the product around water without stating that a resultant electrical shock could cause serious injury or death.

A plaintiff will have a difficult time convincing a jury that he was not aware of your warning if it is conveyed in a way that will grab the user's attention. Many industries and individual manufacturers use warning captions such as DANGER, WARNING, CAUTION or NOTE. Such *hazard intensity labels* are generally a good idea as long as their use is clearly defined and consistently followed. Labels such as DANGER or WARNING should be used for serious hazards that have a relatively high probability of occurring if the instructions are not followed. The use of DANGER where the potential hazard is minimal leaves you susceptible to the claim that your warnings were not credible and could reasonably be ignored.

It is also desirable that you be aware of what your competitors are using as warnings on similar products. It is difficult to defend your warnings successfully if the jury hears that everyone else in the industry uses more precise or more strongly worded warnings.

Marketing the Product   You should also be cognizant of your company's product marketing activity. As explained in Chapter I, representations a company makes about a product (such as through advertising or a guarantee) may be construed by a court as an express warranty. Breach of an express warranty results in liability for any injury caused by the breach. In addition, overpromotion of a product may diminish the effectiveness of any warnings given for the product. All good product liability programs include the mandatory review of all advertising and promotional materials from a product liability perspective.

Contracts With Suppliers and Purchasers   Work with your company's lawyers to ensure that the company's contracts with suppliers and purchasers address product liability issues in ways that limit the company's exposure.

Contractual terms with suppliers can have an important bearing on product liability. If product components are manufactured by other companies, contracts with these suppli-ers should deal with the question of allocation of potential losses from product liability claims and the responsibility for obtaining insurance against such losses. Few things will make your lawyer happier than your producing, at the outset of the lawsuit, a contract between you and the supplier of the allegedly defective component requiring the supplier to indemnify you and provide insurance coverage for all losses arising out of any defects in the component. Depending on the relative bargaining power of the parties, such provisions may be easy to obtain, and they can be invaluable in the event of a lawsuit.

Contractual terms in agreements with purchasers of your product can also have an important impact on your product liability exposure. As noted in Chapter I, contractual provisions disclaiming liability for personal injuries caused by a defective product are regarded as unenforceable throughout the United States. However, if the product is sold to a commercial user, a contract for sale may include terms related to the allocation of losses or terms that disclaim all liability or limit the purchaser's remedies. It is frequently possible, by including a carefully written disclaimer in a sales contract, to limit liability to a commercial buyer for defects in the product sold under the contract. In our experience, most manufacturers' disclaimers are poorly drafted and, as a result, potentially ineffective. Frequently manufacturers do not obtain an effective disclaimer from purchasers because of pressure from their sales forces, which fear that a disclaimer will put them at a competitive disadvantage. Although this is often a valid concern, we suspect that manufacturers sometimes give in too easily on this question.

The effectiveness of these contractual limitations varies from state to state. It is unwise, therefore, to rely entirely on the effectiveness of these provisions. But it is an even greater mistake to fail to make use of them when they might be effective.

All contractual limitations should be in writing and part of the contract of sale. Disclaimers that the buyer never sees until after delivery of the product are always looked on by the courts with disfavor.

The typeface used for the disclaimer should be larger than that used in the rest of the document or should otherwise stand out. The disclaimer provision should have a large-type heading with language that clearly announces its purpose, such as DISCLAIMER, WAIVER AND LIMITATION OF REMEDIES. The language of the provisions should be unambiguous and inclusive. If the intention is to write as broad a disclaimer as possible, then the warranty of fitness, warranty of merchantability, all other implied warranties and all tort liability, including, in particular, negligence and strict liability, should be explicitly mentioned.

There is a federal warranty statute applicable in all states that limits the manufacturer's power to disclaim implied warranties on consumer goods. The requirements are somewhat difficult to understand. If you plan to use disclaimers in connection with consumer goods, you should have a knowledgeable product liability lawyer review your proposed disclaimers before use.

Production Even the best-designed product may prove defective if the production process permits faulty construction. As product liability prevention manager, you should make sure that the company inspects the product at appropriate points in the manufacturing process. For those defects not readily ascertainable through visual inspection, testing procedures may be appropriate.

Your company is the best judge of how and how often one of its products needs to be inspected and tested to see that it conforms to the quality expected. Lawyers can help, however, by ensuring that quality control measures are adequately documented so that the benefits created by a strong quality control program are available to the manufacturer in litigation. Typically, this will involve creating a form that is signed or stamped at various stages of the process. For some products, quantitative measurements may be appropriate. You may want to consider whether qualitative assessments other than "approved" or "passed" should be used. The procedures developed should be simple and straightforward enough so that the forms are completed correctly. It may be better to have no records at all than to have records that are deficient. Thus, your records should be checked for accuracy.

After Delivery of the Product Under the law of many states, a manufacturer must continue to exercise reasonable care to warn consumers of hazards discovered by the manufacturer after the product is delivered. This can be true even if the manufacturer no longer manufactures the product line.

You will reduce your company's exposure to product liability claims by having in place an effective system to accomplish some or all of the following:

➢ *Review the in-service history of the product as known from user communications or from observations by your representatives in the field;*

➢ *Monitor information about the service history of similar products; and*

➢ *Follow changes that may occur in relevant government or industry regulations, standards or practices.*

If information received after delivery of the product leads you to conclude that its original instructions or warnings did not adequately advise the user of a particular hazard, issue updated information using appropriate means to communicate with product users. It is important to have a system to facilitate this communication. Many manufacturers of machinery have service bulletin or service letter procedures to accomplish this. They may also have bulletin or revision services for instructional manuals that describe how to operate and maintain the product. For many manufacturers, especially those that produce consumer goods, the most difficult aspect of developing such a system for issuing post-delivery warnings is keeping track of the identity of the users of the product. Many manufacturers include with the product's instructions a postcard that the purchaser can use to give the company his name and address. If you maintain such records, be sure they are used if a potential hazard is discovered.

In some instances, a newly discovered hazard may prompt you to make a change in the product's design to eliminate the hazard or reduce the possibility of its occurrence or the severity of its consequences. In such a case it may be wise to make current product users aware of the design improvement and to offer a retrofit kit with which they can make the change to their product. Depending on the circumstances and the industry involved, a recall of the product may be the appropriate course of action. A recall typically involves the return of the product for modification or refund.

Consultation with your legal counsel is important to determine your company's obligations when new hazards are discovered after delivery of the product and to formulate the appropriate response.

Insurance The precautions discussed in the preceding sections cannot guarantee that you will not eventually be faced with a product liability lawsuit. For this reason, most manufacturers secure some type of product liability insurance coverage.

Insurance policies designed to protect a business that designs, manufactures and/or sells a product against claims that a defect in the product has harmed a user are available from a variety of sources inside and outside the United States and come in a variety of forms. Advice on how to obtain appropriate insurance coverage on the best terms is far beyond the scope of this primer. What can be done here is to suggest some questions you should ask to be sure that your coverage is tailored to the particular risks you face, and that any limitations on the policy coverage are acceptable in light of the nature of those risks:

➢ *Are the policy's liability limits and the insurer's obligation to provide a defense adequate to protect you in the event a tragic accident occurs while your product is in use? A small component part supplier of a large aircraft can have a huge exposure if the aircraft crashes due to a defect in the part. Defense costs alone in such a case can easily be in the hundreds of thousands of dollars and may total in the millions.*

➢ *Does the policy exclude any type of liability that you are likely to face? Geographic limitations are found in some policies. A manufacturer engaged in export activities generally needs worldwide coverage.*

➢ *Does the policy cover punitive damages? Some policies expressly exclude punitive damages, while others never address the question.*

➢ *Does the policy give you a voice in the selection of counsel? Many American companies have found it useful to appoint law firms as national or regional trial counsel for specific product lines or areas of the country. The advantage is that the lawyers develop expertise in your product, come to know your key employees and do not need to traverse a learning curve with every new claim. This system also assures that you are represented by competent counsel.*

It is advisable to review insurance coverages, particularly liability limits and exclusions, on a regular basis to ensure that the protection afforded continues to be adequate and comprehensive as your business grows and changes over time. Sound insurance planning carried out before a claim arises can be one of the most important assets of your defense in a product liability lawsuit.

Between Accident and Lawsuit

Learning of Accidents   Ideally, you should have knowledgeable people investigate each significant accident involving your product soon after the accident occurs and before the physical evidence has been destroyed. Unfortunately, before you can investigate an accident, you first have to learn that the accident has occurred. Learning of accidents involving your products can be easy or it can be very difficult.

In the aviation area, for example, governments have programs for investigating most aircraft accidents and incidents, and airframe and engine manufacturers generally learn of serious accidents involving their products within hours of the occurrence. However, in many industries, it is usually difficult to obtain timely notice about product-related accidents unless the accidents capture headlines.

Consider what kind of system is best for learning about serious accidents involving the company's products. Newspaper clipping services are available, and so are distributor and dealer networks. The system must be tailored to the your company's circumstances.

There is no reason to have a system for learning of accidents if you do not also have a system for constructively using the knowledge you obtain. If your intelligence-gathering activities result only in the creation of files full of third-hand, negative reports about the performance of a product under unspecified conditions, all that has been accomplished is the collection of documents that plaintiffs will use against you in their lawsuits. Moreover, attorneys have been known to contact persons involved in such reported incidents and solicit their claims.

Investigation   If you decide to investigate serious accidents involving your products, you need trained investigators with the following qualities:

➤ *Familiarity with the product;*

➤ *A good common-sense understanding of what is important in determining how an accident occurred;*

➤ *Sufficient familiarity with lawsuits to be sensitive to evidentiary problems;*

➤ *Personality characteristics conducive to being a good witness, because the investigator will undoubtedly be called to testify on behalf of the company on many occasions; and*

➤ *Most importantly, a high energy level and a strong sense of commitment to the product and the company.*

Accident investigators should be selected carefully. In some companies the job has been regarded as a dead end. It should not be. In pay, status and career opportunities, management should make it clear that accident investigators are valuable employees. People who are simply putting in their time until retirement are not likely to exhibit the creativity and energy needed in a good accident investigator. Beyond that, because the job involves working closely with lawyers, it is important to have people who can and will work well with them.

There are two primary purposes of an early investigation. First, and more importantly, your company must learn what caused the accident to see if there is a product problem that needs to be remedied. Second, the facts and circumstances of the accident should be documented so that a record can be preserved for later use in defending a lawsuit. Always be careful, however, that the investigation is not handled in such a way that it precipitates a claim that would not otherwise have been made.

Also consider how best to document the results of an investigation. Some companies create two reports: information needed for the company's purposes is reported through normal company channels, and information gathered for litigation purposes goes directly to the company's lawyers and is not distributed within the company. This lets you deal with any product problems that may have been detected during the investigation and ensure that attorney-client or work-product privilege protects the other information.

Informal Claim Handling   Sometimes claims with the potential for developing into lawsuits can be appropriately and fairly resolved at an early stage. Compared to the costs of litigation, there might be many things that your company can offer an informal claimant that prove cost-effective in the long run. The key is an informal claim handling program staffed with people who are cordial and diligent, so that the claimant does not develop a sense of anger and outrage that may cause him to sue.

When Lawyers Are Involved   When a claimant's lawyer is involved in presenting the claim, the opportunities for a quick, reasonable settlement are often diminished but not necessarily eliminated. The initial claim may come from a lawyer who is a friend or business acquaintance of the claimant and who has not entered into a contingent-fee agreement with the claimant. (A contingent-fee lawyer is one who takes a plaintiff's case on the basis that if he loses he gets no fee and if he wins will be paid a percentage of the award granted to the plaintiff, usually 30 to 40 percent.) In that situation you may be able to show the claimant the value of settling the claim early so that the entire recovery is his (less modest hourly charges to the lawyer), rather than having to share 30 or 40 percent of the award with a contingent-fee lawyer.

Sometimes a manufacturer is contacted by a lawyer representing an injured person in litigation with a third party who is looking for information about the product to use in that litigation. Dealing with such requests is a tricky problem. If you are uncooperative and tell him that you will give him no assistance, this may result in your company being named as a party in the lawsuit. But it is generally not a wise policy to turn over access to company documents and personnel without restriction. When this situation arises, the best course may be to start off by simply asking the attorney directly if he is considering asserting a claim against the company. If the lawyer indicates that a claim is not being considered, you should ask for a release in exchange for your cooperation.

Whenever the claimant or potential claimant has involved a lawyer, you should have one involved on behalf of the company. Most nonlawyers cannot be expected to understand the legal system well enough to avoid getting into trouble when negotiating with lawyers.

Defending Lawsuits

Receipt of the Complaint Your company should have a system for dealing with a complaint promptly when it is received. Litigation papers cannot be allowed to gather dust on someone's desk or travel from office to office in search of a final resting place. There are a number of reasons why this is important. First, as previously discussed, the company can be in default if it fails to answer the complaint within the time period established by the court. A court may excuse a default entered as a result of the company's inability to get the complaint to the right people in time to file an answer, but the adverse consequence of a default judgment is so great that you cannot afford to take this chance. Second, a right to remove the action from state to federal court may be lost if the complaint is not dealt with promptly. If there is more than one defendant, all must join in the removal notice, and it requires some advance planning to do that in a timely manner. Finally, a long delay in dealing with the complaint may restrict your ability to hire the lawyer you want. In small communities, there may be only a few lawyers capable of representing you adequately in product litigation. A delay in reacting to the complaint may result in the best lawyers having been hired by others.

Reliance on Insurers Most product liability insurance policies have provisions giving the insurer the right to control the defense, including the choice of defense counsel. If your policy has such provisions, one question that you should address is whether the insurer will consult with you when choosing counsel. The most successful product liability prevention programs are those in which the company is deeply involved in cooperation with the insurer, even in activities that the insurance company has a right to control. In cases involving serious accidents or significant financial exposure, you may want to recommend a lawyer or law firm to your insurers, choosing them not because of their rates, but rather for their ability and track record in handling complicated product liability matters. When serious litigation is on the horizon, you should choose your defense lawyers the same way you would choose a brain surgeon—very carefully.

If your company and its insurers are confronted with many product liability suits, it may be advisable to have a single law firm coordinate claims on a national basis or to use several law firms with regional responsibilities. This approach avoids many of the difficulties of educating a lot of local lawyers regarding technical issues relating to the product.

Litigation Support An important part of any product liability program is assisting your lawyers in defending product liability litigation. This assistance generally has two aspects. First, the company should have a "litigation support" staff to gather documents, find witnesses and generally help your lawyers respond to discovery and prepare the case for trial. Generally the qualities that should be looked for in litigation support personnel are thoroughness, imagination and knowledge about the company and its products. Of these, thoroughness and imagination are clearly the most important, because knowledge can be acquired over time. Those selected must each be a "can-do" type of person who will respond promptly and completely to your lawyers' requests for assistance and who can make helpful suggestions to them as to what information useful to the defense might be available. People whose normal reaction to a request for assistance is to explain why the request cannot be complied with are not appropriate for this work.

The litigation support people may be the same people who investigate accidents. Although this is typically the case, there are some disadvantages to this system. As already noted, the investigators will undoubtedly have their depositions taken during the pretrial discovery phase. If these same persons are the litigation support people, they may have substantially more information about the case as a result of those activities than what they learned from their investigation activities. The results of their investigation will generally be discoverable by the plaintiff. Much of the litigation support work done at the request of the lawyers is not. But it is difficult to restrict a witness to testifying only about the knowledge acquired through an accident investigation in the remote past and not about present knowledge that has been augmented by litigation support activities. In other words, using the same people for investigation and litigation support may result in the disclosure of information developed for your lawyers and provide plaintiffs some insight into the defense strategy.

Even more important than having people whose formal duties include litigation support is having, throughout your entire organization, a clearly understood policy of doing what is needed to support its litigation efforts. Many companies do not adequately support their lawyers. Invariably, they learn the hard way that these claims are extremely important and their outcomes can have not only direct monetary consequences, but a significant impact on how the public views their products.

Settling Cases Most product liability claims are settled before they get to trial. As a general rule, plaintiffs' lawyers working on a contingent-fee basis find it more profitable to settle cases than try them, for the simple reason that they can settle many claims in the time it takes to complete one trial. Where it is likely that a defect in your product caused a claimant's injury, it usually makes sense for you to want an early settlement, too.

In spite of this, lawsuits drag on for years, frequently to settle on the courthouse steps after significant legal fees and expenses have accumulated. The lawyers or insurers are usually to blame. There are many reasons for last-minute settlements, including inertia, overwork, unrealistic assessment of liability or damages, competing egos and greed.

Many books have been written about negotiating settlements, but here are a few useful rules we have learned:

➤ *The value of cases escalates over time. If it is probable that a product defect caused the claimant's injury, you will probably save money by settling early, and you will certainly save legal fees and the disruption of your business caused by litigation.*

➤ *One reason cases take a long time to settle is that the lawyers for one or more of the parties do not understand the merits (or lack thereof) of their case. Therefore it is often useful to educate your opponent and make him focus on the merits of his case. A motion for summary judgment often has this therapeutic effect even if the motion is ultimately denied.*

➤ *Lawyers are gladiators; they like to fight. That may be what you want them to do, but often it isn't. At an early date you should make clear to your lawyer what your goals are. This may sound obvious, but it often isn't. Many lawyers go after each other with hammer and tongs because the manufacturer or insurer has failed to tell anyone that it would be very happy with a nice, quiet, reasonable, prompt settlement.*

➤ Egos frequently get in the way of settlements. Sometimes a lawsuit develops a life of its own unrelated to the objectives of the parties. It is useful from time to time to pause and examine whether egos and combative instincts are prolonging the battle.

➤ It is important to get a handle on the facts of the case as soon as possible. If you have a problem in a lawsuit (for example, some bad documents) and your lawyer learns of the problem early on and before the plaintiff's lawyer does, it may be possible to negotiate a more reasonable settlement than would be possible once the problem becomes public knowledge. Again, this may sound obvious, but we have seen many lawsuits in which a manufacturer failed to inform its lawyer of soft spots in its defense until it was too late.

➤ The strength of a defense changes over time and it is important not to be blinded by your early assessment of the merits of the case. It is valuable to reassess the case periodically. As the discovery process proceeds and new facts come to light, it may be time to reevaluate what you are willing to pay in settlement. You don't have to wait until you get to the courthouse steps to abandon that early optimistic assessment.

➤ It is best to litigate each case as aggressively as you can right up to the day that it settles. Most good settlements are achieved simply by being better prepared and getting your side into a better position in the litigation than the other side.

CONCLUSION

Our purpose in writing this primer was not to help manufacturers of defective products win lawsuits. Those claims are best settled early and fairly. However, many manufacturers have been burned by the American product liability system in cases where, in their heart of hearts, they knew their product was not defective and that they had not done anything wrong.

Our experience defending product liability lawsuits and working closely with manufacturers on product liability prevention programs convinces us that manufacturers can lessen their product liability exposure significantly in such cases by properly educating their employees. This primer can be used to provide employees with an understanding of the basics of product liability law (Chapter I), the procedures involved in product liability lawsuits (Chapter II) and the preventive measures that can be taken to reduce product liability exposure (Chapter III). Hopefully, it can reduce the number of instances where the legal system backfires and punishes a manufacturer undeservedly.

SAMPLE JURY INSTRUCTIONS

(Drawn from standard California jury instructions. These instructions, together with others, will be read by the judge to the jury at the close of the case.)

In this case plaintiff seeks to establish liability on the part of the defendant on one or more of three different claimed bases of recovery.

Strict Liability

The first is the claim that the product in question was defective. I will now instruct on the law as it relates to the claim of a defective product.

Manufacturing Defect

The manufacturer of a product is liable for injuries a proximate cause of which was a defect in its manufacture which existed when it left possession of the manufacturer, provided that the injury resulted from a use of the product that was reasonably foreseeable by the manufacturer.

A defect in the manufacture of a product exists if the product differs from the manufacturer's intended result or if the product differs from apparently identical products from the same manufacturer.

Design Defect

The manufacturer of a product is liable for injuries proximately caused by a defect in its design which existed when it left the possession of the manufacturer provided that they resulted from a use of the product that was reasonably foreseeable by the manufacturer.

A product is defective in design: if it fails to perform as safely as an ordinary consumer would expect when used in an intended or reasonably foreseeable manner, or if there is a risk of danger inherent in the design which outweighs the benefits of that design.

In determining whether the benefits of the design outweigh such risks you may consider, among other things, the gravity of the danger posed by the design, the likelihood that such danger would cause damage, the mechanical feasibility of a safer alternate design at the time of manufacture, the financial cost of an improved design, and the adverse consequences to the product and the consumer that would result from an alternate design.

Warning Defect

A product is defective if the use of the product in a manner that is reasonably foreseeable by the defendant involves a substantial danger that would not be readily recognized by the ordinary user of the product and the manufacturer fails to give adequate warning of such danger.

Negligence

The second claimed basis of recovery is the claim that the defendant was negligent in the manufacture of the product in question. I will now instruct you on the law as it relates to the claim of negligence in the manufacture of a product.

The manufacturer of a product that is reasonably certain to be dangerous if negligently made has a duty to exercise reasonable care in the design, manufacture, testing and inspection of the product and in the testing and inspection of any component parts made by another so that the product may be safely used in a manner and for a purpose for which it was made.

A failure to fulfill that duty is negligence.

Breach of Warranty

The third claimed basis of recovery is the claim that the defendant breached a warranty with respect to the product in question. I will now instruct you on the law as it relates to the claim of breach of warranty. A breach of warranty may be established without proof of negligence on the part of the defendant.

One of the elements of a sale of a product may be an affirmation of fact or promise by the manufacturer that the product possesses certain characteristics. Such an affirmation of fact or promise is called a warranty. It may be made expressly in so many words by the seller or it may be implied from the circumstances of the sale.

The term "affirmation of fact" means a positive assertion of a fact or statement concerning the subject matter of a transaction, which might otherwise be only an expression of opinion, which is affirmed as an existing fact material to the transaction and reasonably induces the other party to rely upon it as fact.

Express Warranty

Any affirmation of fact made by the seller to the buyer which relates to the product and becomes part of the basis of the bargain creates an express warranty that the product shall conform to the affirmation or promise. Such affirmation or promise may be oral or in writing.

Any description of the goods which is made part of the basis of the bargain creates an express warranty that the goods shall conform to the description.

Any sample or model which is made part of the basis of the bargain creates an express warranty that the whole of the goods shall conform to the sample or model.

No particular word or form of expression is necessary to create an express warranty, nor is it necessary that the seller use formal words such as "warrant" or "guarantee" or that he have a specific intention to make a warranty.

Implied Warranty

Where the seller at the time of the sale has reason to know any particular purpose for which the goods are required and that the buyer is relying on the seller's skill or judgment to select or furnish suitable goods, there is an implied warranty that the goods shall be fit for such purpose.

In a sale of goods such as that which occurred in this case, there is an implied warranty that the goods shall be merchantable. By this is meant that the goods are at least fit for the ordinary purposes for which such goods are used.

Proximate Cause

A "proximate cause" of injury is a cause which, in natural and continuous sequence, produces the injury and without which the injury would not have occurred.

GLOSSARY

This glossary provides simplified definitions of various terms as they are used in the context of product liability lawsuits.

Affirmative defense A defense that must be asserted in the *defendant's answer* and that, if proven, will eliminate or lessen *defendant's liability* to the *plaintiff*

Answer The document in which the *defendant* responds to the *plaintiff's complaint*

Appellate court A court which reviews decisions of a trial court

Bench trial A trial without a *jury*

Bifurcation Separate trials of different issues in the same lawsuit, such as *liability* and *damages*

Breach of warranty Violation of a *warranty*

Burden of proof The obligation of a party to a lawsuit to persuade the *jury*, or the judge in a *bench trial*, that a fact is more likely true than not true

Challenge for cause A request that a prospective juror not be allowed to be a member of the *jury* because of specified reasons

Class action A lawsuit in which the *plaintiff* asserts claims on behalf of a class of similarly situated people

Closing argument The final statements made by the lawyers to the *jury* (or to the judge in a *bench trial*)

Collateral source Compensation for an injury received by the *plaintiff* from a source wholly independent of the *defendant*

Comparative fault Relative fault of those who caused the *plaintiff's* injury

Comparative negligence Relative *negligence* of those who caused the *plaintiff's* injury

Compensatory damages *Damages* to compensate the *plaintiff* for *economic* and *noneconomic losses*

Complaint The document that describes the *plaintiff's* claims and is filed with the court and delivered to the *defendant* in order to start a lawsuit

Contingent fee A percentage (usually 30 to 40 percent) of the amount awarded the *plaintiff* that is paid to the lawyer who successfully argued the case

Contribution The right of one who has paid a common *liability* to recover a portion of the payment from another who is also *liable*

Contributory negligence *Negligence* of the *plaintiff* that was a cause of his injury

Counterclaim A claim by a *defendant* against the *plaintiff*

Cross-claim A claim by one *defendant* against another *defendant*

Cross-examination Questioning of a witness by the lawyer for a party opposed to the one who called the witness to testify at trial

Damages The monetary compensation that may be awarded by a court to a person who has suffered an injury

Default judgment A *judgment* entered against a *defendant* who has failed to respond to the *plaintiff's complaint*

Defendant The party to a lawsuit from whom the *plaintiff* seeks to recover *damages*

Deponent A witness who testifies at a *deposition*

Deposition A method of pretrial *discovery* in which a person is questioned orally under oath and a record is made of the questions and answers

Direct examination Questioning of a witness by the lawyer for the party that called the witness to testify at trial

Directed verdict A *verdict* ordered by the judge because the *plaintiff* failed to present sufficient evidence for the *jury* to find against the *defendant*

Disclaimer A contract provision in which one party renounces its right to make certain claims against another party to the contract

Discovery The pretrial procedures by which a party to a lawsuit can obtain information from another party to the lawsuit or from others

Diversity jurisdiction *Jurisdiction* of federal courts to hear cases between citizens of different states or between a citizen of one state and a citizen of a foreign country

Document request A request by one party during pretrial *discovery* to inspect and/or copy documents or other tangible items in the possession, custody or control of another party

Economic losses Monetary losses and out-of-pocket expenses such as lost earnings and medical expenses

Expert witness A witness who by reason of education or experience possesses scientific, technical or other specialized knowledge that will assist the *jury* to understand the evidence or determine a factual issue

FMEA Failure Mode and Effect Analysis that identifies all possible failures of a product and determines the consequences of each

Forum non conveniens The discretionary power of a court to decline *jurisdiction* over a lawsuit when the convenience of parties and witnesses and the ends of justice would be better served if the lawsuit were brought and tried in another state or nation

General verdict A *verdict* in which the *jury* finds for either the *plaintiff* or *defendant* in general terms

Interrogatories A method of pretrial *discovery* in which one party to the lawsuit asks questions in writing to another party to the lawsuit

Joint and several liability The *liability* of two or more persons who caused the *plaintiff's* injury to pay the entire amount of *damages* awarded

Judgment The final decision of the court resolving a lawsuit and determining the rights and obligations of the parties

Jurisdiction The power of a particular court to decide a case because it has authority over the parties to and the subject matter of the lawsuit

Jury The group of citizens who hear evidence and decide disputed facts in a lawsuit

Jury demand A request by a party to a lawsuit to have a trial by *jury*

Liability An obligation to pay *damages*

Liable Obligated to pay *damages*

Litigation A lawsuit

Misuse Use of a product that is not in accord with the manufacturer's intended use

Motion to dismiss An alternative to filing an *answer,* and a way to raise a defense easily presented, such as lack of *jurisdiction*, at the outset of the lawsuit

Negligence   The failure to exercise the degree of care that a reasonable person would exercise under the same circumstances

Noneconomic losses Nonfinancial hardships, such as pain and suffering

Objection A statement by a lawyer that a question to a witness or a request during *discovery* is improper

Opening statement The initial statements by the lawyers to the *jury* (or to the judge in a *bench trial*) describing the nature of the lawsuit and the anticipated proof

Peremptory challenge The right to excuse a prospective juror without giving a reason

Personal injury Harm to one's person

Personal jurisdiction   The power of a court over a defendant who resides or engages in purposeful activity in the court's territory

Plaintiff   The party to a lawsuit who seeks an award of *damages* from the *defendant* and who starts the lawsuit by filing a *complaint*

Privilege   A protection against forced disclosures of confidential communications between lawyers and clients and between others in certain protected relationships

Product liability   The *liability* of the manufacturer or others in the chain of distribution of a product to a person injured by the use of the product

Protective order   A court order protecting a party to a lawsuit from an improper request during pretrial *discovery*

Punitive damages   *Damages* awarded not to compensate the *plaintiff* but to punish the *defendant* and deter the *defendant* and others from future misconduct

Rebuttal evidence   Evidence presented during trial by a party after he has *rested* his case and after the opposing party has *rested* in order to contradict the opposing party's evidence

Removal   A transfer of a lawsuit from state court to federal court

Rests   Finishes presenting evidence at trial, either finally or subject to a right to present *rebuttal evidence*

Service   Delivery of court papers

Special verdict   A *verdict* in which the *jury* answers specific questions

Statute of limitations   A law that fixes the length of time after an injury during which a lawsuit may be filed

Statute of repose A law that fixes the length of time after initial delivery of the product during which a lawsuit may be filed

Strict liability *Liability* of the manufacturer or others in the chain of distribution of the product to a person injured as a result of a defective condition in the product

Subject matter jurisdiction The power of a particular court to decide a lawsuit because it has authority over the subject matter of the lawsuit

Summary judgment Resolution of a lawsuit (or a portion of it) by the judge without a trial where there is no dispute regarding the facts

Summons A document delivered to the *defendant* to give initial notice that the lawsuit has been started and that the *defendant* must respond to the *plaintiff's complaint* by filing an *answer*

Survival action A lawsuit for claims that a person could have made up to the time of his death but did not

Third-party claim A claim by a *defendant* against a person who is neither a *plaintiff* nor another *defendant* in the lawsuit

Third-party defendant The person against whom a *third-party claim* is made

Venue The district or political subdivision in which a court with *jurisdiction* may hear and determine a lawsuit

Verdict The decision of the *jury*

Voir dire Questioning of prospective jurors by the judge and lawyers to determine their qualifications and suitability to serve as jurors

Warranty An express or implied promise that the product sold has certain qualities

Wrongful death action A lawsuit by or on behalf of surviving family members and other heirs for losses they have suffered or will suffer as a result of a death

INDEX

Softbound copies of this primer are available from Perkins Coie for $9.95 each, including shipping and handling. To order, or to be included on a mailing list for future revisions, simply complete this form and mail it to this address:

Perkins Coie
Attention: Product Liability Practice Group
1201 Third Avenue, 40th Floor
Seattle, WA 98101-3099

Please send me _____ softbound copies of *Product Liability in the United States: A Primer for Manufacturers and Their Employees* at $9.95 per copy. My check for $_____ is enclosed (U.S. funds).

Name _____

Title _____

Company _____

Address _____

City/State/Zip _____

Country/Zip/Postal Code _____

Phone _____